The Promise
of a New Day

The Promise of a New Day

by
Karen Casey
and
Martha Vanceburg

Hazelden
Always, the pioneer

Box 176
Center City, MN 55012

First printing, October, 1983

© Copyright, 1983, Hazelden Foundation. All rights reserved. No portion of this book may be reproduced without written permission of the publisher.

ISBN: 0-89486-204-9

Printed in the United States of America.

About the authors:
Karen Casey's successful first book, *Each Day A New Beginning,* inspired this one. Although writing is her first love, Karen has also taught in elementary school and in college, and has been a publishing executive. Karen has a Ph.D. in American studies. She is married and lives in Minneapolis.

Martha Vanceburg has worked in theater, advertising, public relations, publishing, and academia, but prefers writing. She has three children and has been married to her best critic for twenty-seven years.

About the illustrator:
David Spohn lives in Chisago City with his wife, two sons, and two elderly cats. His work has appeared in publications and shows throughout Minnesota.

INTRODUCTION

It takes strength to step enthusiastically into each day of our lives. This strength comes more readily on some days than on others, but every day makes demands on us.

Personal experience has taught us that centering ourselves in the face of these demands smooths our passage. To get centered means to sense our place in the grand scheme and to trust the rightness of all experiences that beckon.

It is our hope that these brief daily meditations will help you find your place, and thus help you summon the forces to see you through the days ahead. We both follow a Twelve Step program for sane living, and openness is an integral part of this approach. Healing, help, and wisdom may come from anywhere, so we gathered these quotations from men and women of many lands and times, and let them stimulate our own reflections.

Taking responsibility for our own lives, trusting in the rightness of a plan—however we may define the higher power that is its source, and nurturing ourselves to be the best we can; these are the tasks that renew our energies even as we perform them.

The words we have chosen remind us that women and men in every place and time have pondered, struggled, succeeded, and failed in much the same way as we. In every case, they had the drive to begin their journeys anew, day after day. They are like all of us. We are like all of them: journeying forth courageously one day, tentatively the next. The real importance of the journey is simply that we're making it, alone and yet mysteriously together.

The authors

January

One faces the future with one's past.
—*Pearl S. Buck*

We are never divorced from our past. We are in company with it forever, and it acquaints us with the present. Our responses today reflect our experiences yesterday. And those roots lie in the past.

Every day is offering us preparation for the future, for the lessons to come, without which we'd not offer our full measure to the design which contains the development of us all.

Our experiences, past and present, are not coincidental. We will be introduced to those experiences that are consistent with our talents and the right lessons designated for the part we are requested to play in life. We can remember that no experiences will attract us that are beyond our capabilities to handle.

All is well. I'm ready for whatever comes today. My yesterdays have prepared me.

January 2

*One cannot collect all the beautiful shells
on the beach, one can collect only a few.*
— *Anne Morrow Lindbergh*

Our lives are a series of selections. We select projects to do, activities to participate in, friendships to cultivate. And often we'll have to forego some of the selections we've made because time and energy run out. Full commitment, total involvement with singular activities and few friendships is far better than partial attention to many. Rapt attention to the moment and all of whatever it contains enriches our lives; nothing less than full attention can do so.

The talents we each have been blessed with can only be developed if we use them fully to benefit the lives of others as well as our own. Thus, when our selections are vast, our attention is sporadic and our talents aren't fully developed. The fullness of our lives individually and collectively is proportionate to the depth of the relationships developed between ourselves, our friends, and our activities.

I can't be everywhere today. Nor can I attend to the needs of everybody I meet. I will carefully choose where to give my attention and then offer it totally.

. . . goodness cannot adopt the form of blind
passions, even in the act of defense and offense,
and even when it refuses to tolerate evil . . .
— *Benedetto Croce*

Willful blindness can't be good. To shut out any sight from the mind's eye is to exclude part of life. Any action blindly taken is likely to do unintentional harm.

It's not easy, when we're in the grip of any strong feeling, to stop ourselves from acting on blind impulse. It's not easy, but it's wise. Yielding to an impulse, without giving ourselves time to "see" it through clearly, can set us up for guilt or regret.

We needn't know everything in order to act; we merely need to know ourselves. "Blind passion" hides most of ourselves from view. Passion may move us to great selflessness, but never to great clarity, and good actions come from the clear-seeing soul.

I can trust myself to mistrust blind passion, and to wait for clarity before I take action.

January 4

> *Faith is not, contrary to the usual ideas,*
> *something that turns out to be right or wrong,*
> *like a gambler's bet; it's an act, an intention,*
> *a project, something that makes you, in leap-*
> *ing into the future, go so far, far, far ahead*
> *that you shoot clean out of time and right*
> *into Eternity, which is not the end of time*
> *or a whole lot of time or unending time, but*
> *timelessness, that old Eternal Now.*
> —Joanna Russ

Isn't it amazing how some people contrive to live in the present? They seem not to worry about the future; they seem not to regret the past. "Two days I can't do anything about," runs the saying, "yesterday and tomorrow."

We love to fantasize about the past and the future: What if Napoleon had died in infancy? Where would I travel in a time machine? But we get into trouble when we forget that "the past" and "the future" are inventions; the only reality is the present. Yes, past events contribute to our now; yes, the present will help to determine the future. But we can't do anything about them; they are out of our reach.

It seems, oddly enough, that it's people with a strong faith who are best able to live in the present moment. Enjoyment of the present; care for the quality of life; these are a kind of reverence, a kind of faith in life itself. The present is valuable, this faith tells us: it is all we have.

Let me swim in the present, reverential and unafraid.
Let me be sustained by the water of life.

*Nothing on earth consumes a man more
completely than the passion of resentment.*
— *Friedrich Nietzsche*

Our obsession with controlling other people,
and our failure to succeed with our attempts,
most likely consistent attempts, is the fodder
for the resentments that we garner. It's human
to want to control others; to try to control outcomes to favor us. But the resentment that
develops begins controlling us, and this situation leads only to frustration, at times panic,
always unhappiness.

If we're feeling resentment toward anyone,
or because of any situation, we are not able to
recognize the opportunities presenting themselves to us today. And when we don't respond
to the invitations for meaningful involvement,
our personal growth is jeopardized.

We give our power away when resentment
swallows us. Our identity becomes enmeshed
with it. Responsible action eludes us. Fortunately, we can take back our power just as soon
as we decide to get free of the resentment.

*The lesson I must learn is simply that my control is limited
to my own behavior, my own attitudes. Today can be my
new beginning.*

January 6

It is not what we see and touch or that which others do for us which makes us happy; it is that which we think and feel and do, first for the other fellow and then for ourselves.
—Helen Keller

Our attention to someone else's needs is spirit-lifting, both for that someone and for ourselves. We need to move our focus away from the self to experience our well-deserved emotional health. The more frequently we honor another person's needs above our own, the greater will be our own strides along the path to health and wholeness.

When we peer beyond ourselves, we remove our attention from whatever our present personal problem is and it dies from neglect. We keep a problem a problem when we indulge it by obsessing over it. Switching our focus offers a perspective that's new, and thus destined to be beneficial.

All around me today are people whose needs are greater than my own. Personal health is enhanced when I forget myself.

*I'm not sorry for anyone's being poor; I'm
only sorry when they have no work.*
—Helena Morley

Human beings have been described as animals
with language, animals with laughter, tool-
using animals, animals that play. But we're pre-
eminently animals that work. Small children's
play is imitation of the work they see adults
doing. Fortunate adults put the same energy and
devotion into their work as children do into
their play.

Work—although we sometimes curse it—is
a blessing. Work, the work that is a real expression of the spirit, focuses our energy and allows
us to be whole. Maybe our real work isn't our
job; maybe we feel whole when we're carpen-
tering or cooking or writing, and we think of
these as "hobbies" or "just stuff I do." If we
could bring to our jobs the concentration and
pride with which we turn a chair leg or roll up
sticky buns, we would exalt our working days.

The jobs we do, the work for which we're
paid, are deeply important to most of us. When
we find work we can love, and do it as well as
we're able, we've earned a victory in life.

*I will try to be able to say of my work today, "I would do
this even if I weren't paid for it."*

January 8

*All writers are vain, selfish and lazy, and
at the very bottom of their motives there lies
a mystery.*

—*George Orwell*

For the most part, we receive too much information. We're bombarded with print, sound, images. Many of us cultivate a healthy skepticism: we consider the source. What does this person, this agency, this network, this advertiser, or this elected official stand to gain from telling me this information?

But we cannot doubt everything. Humans need to believe in something, even something wildly implausible on the face of it. Thus, cults and causes abound. In this age of widespread corruption and cynicism, faith also is widespread.

Faith is healthy; it is an affirmation of human worth and continuity. Fortunate are those of us who have both strong faith and good judgment. Belief in the essential goodness of our fellows and in the basic rightness of our world can renew our vitality and remind us to treat others with the respect due their humanity. In turn, others will respect our belief in them.

Sometimes, faith is betrayed; sometimes, we stumble. But the delusions or mistakes of others need not sour us; they are part of the mystery.

*I will believe in my own capacity for goodness, and all
will be well.*

When a man leaves off believing in imaginary property, then only will he make use of his true property.

—*Leo Tolstoy*

The original meaning of property is "belonging to the self." In this sense, land, houses, money, paintings, jewels, cars, cannot be our *property;* they are all things, and we enjoy using them, but they have nothing to do with our *selves.*

What then is our true property? It's our moral and spiritual qualities; our capacity for love, our commitment to honesty. These are what make a difference in who we are. The difference between a lie and the truth is vastly greater than the difference between a bicycle and a Mercedes. When we appreciate this distinction, we can begin to develop our spiritual selves.

We all know that things can't make us happy; only a loving heart and a clear conscience can do that. Yet often we act as though the piling up of things were important in itself. A little reflection can restore our balance and return our imaginary property to its true place in our lives.

True property is what nothing can take away from me.

January 10

> *A private railroad car is not an acquired*
> *taste. One takes to it immediately.*
> —*Eleanor R. Belmont*

The hunger for solitude visits each of us at various points in our development as whole, healthy human beings. It's in our solitude that we come to know ourselves, to appreciate the many nuances that distinguish us from others. It's in the stillness that we detect our soul's inclinations. The privacy of silence offers us the answers we need. The distractions that stood in our way no longer fetter us when we've invited solitude to be our guest.

We need time away from others, from the chaos of our job, families, and society if we are to find, once again, the clarity we need to make the best forward movement. We cannot hear "The Director" call to us when all around is the clatter of voices and anxiety.

I will relish the moments of silence today. They'll reward me with sure guidance and clarity of thought.

*Children require guidance and sympathy
far more than instruction.*
                              —*Anne Sullivan*

Children are not just the people under ten.
We are all children at heart. And in many of the
activities that call us we are as uncertain of the
steps to take, as unsure of the outcomes' course,
as any ten-year-old. No matter the age, what
we all need in the midst of any challenge is soft
comfort from a loved one and gentle probing
questions that serve to guide our choices as we
move ahead with the task.

Giving someone explicit directions about how
to proceed can deprive them of opportunities
for discovery. Stumbling is part of the human
experience. Picking ourselves up allows us an
additional glance at the landscape on which we
tripped. In the second glance comes a new understanding and thus the growth the gift of life
has promised us.

*I'll comfort another child today and willingly accept the
guidance offered by my own mentor.*

January 12

Freedom means choosing your burden.
                    —*Hephzibah Menuhin*

Every one of us is haunted by fears of some measure. That we learn through pain and grow beyond our fears we can only appreciate in retrospect. During the moment of painful confrontation or the spell of overwhelming anxiety we learn only that we're feeling no joy, no peace, and probably no security. However, we must remember that no painful burden, be it immobilizing anxiety or a relationship in which we've become victimized, has "happened" to us without acceptance—no matter how passive. We are free to reject all burdens and all unhealthy conditions. That we don't relish our freedom from all pain is a fact of the human condition.

Looking anew at the struggles that confound us and accepting responsibility for them doesn't lessen them, perhaps, but it does restore our personal power. We are not powerless, worthless individuals at the mercy of our friends and co-workers. We are in partnership all the way, and any moment we each have the power to rewrite the terms of the contract.

I am free today to be who I want to be. To grow or not to grow. To feel joy or pain.

*Our reality is influenced by our notions
about reality, regardless of the nature of
those notions.*

—Joseph Chilton Pearce

How we greet today will color the returns of
this day. Further, our expectations will be mani-
fest, which means we have the personal power
to determine the course our minds and thus our
actions will take. It's both awesome and thrilling
to understand that we are each responsible for
our affairs. Moreover, we will handle them with
ease or experience turmoil as is our habit.

What we perceive at any moment is equal to
our vision of that moment. If we want more
laughter, greater freedom, further attainments,
they lie within our power—they can't elude us
unless we let them. But first we must define
our direction for movement and then coach our
steps along the way.

*I go where I want to go. I see what I want to see. Every-
thing can change in a flash of the mind's eye.*

January 14

Perhaps this very instant is your time . . .
your own, your peculiar, your promised and
presaged moment, out of all moments for-
ever.

—Louise Bogan

"This very instant" is all we have. We make plans for the future, we invoke memories of the past, but really, all we have to deal with and to act in is the moment at hand. We cannot stop its going; we cannot hurry the next moment on its way. Like everyone else in the world, we're partners in the dull, humdrum, dazzling, fabulous, totally unpredictable moment.

And if we have a time that is "our time," it's right now. It has to be, because there isn't any other. Maybe we've had times in the past that were special for us; maybe the future will hold precious moments. But the only time that is truly "our time" is this time, where we are, right now. And what we do with this time is ours to decide.

Each moment is mine, to make as beautiful or as painful as I choose.

When the most important things in our life
happen we quite often do not know, at the
moment, what is going on.
                                        —C. S. Lewis

Retrospect offers us what no one moment,
in the present, is capable of doing. There is a
pattern to the events of our lives, and even what
appear as the most inconsequential occurrences
are contributing their input to the larger picture that's developing. There is no question
but that every event has meaning. No experience is without its impact. Time will reveal the
reason for the baffling or troubling situations
that have dogged our paths along the way.

Whenever the road feels rocky or we are con-
fused, we need to trust. Our lives are not happenstance. There is a performance being staged.

How helpful it is to understand that we are
all "players" sharing the same stage. All of us
are needed for some acts, and there will be a con-
cluding scene making clear the intricacies of
our many earlier scenes. As life progresses, our
understanding grows. Our finales are assuredly
appropriate to our life plan.

Today's happenings will have their impact. Sometime—
in some way. All moments, all events are part of my
sacred pathway.

January 16

*We are partakers of a common nature, and
the same causes that contribute to the benefit
of one contribute to the benefit of another.*
— William Godwin

Ecology, the study of how all life fits together,
has an emotional dimension. We all know people
who are emotional polluters. Bullies, gossips,
or self-pitiers spread a noxious influence; no
one wants to be around them.

Often they're gifted people, and sometimes
they're in positions of power over others. It's
difficult to keep our own clarity among the
belching smokestacks of an emotional polluter.
But our ecology—our interconnectedness—
means that, potentially, we influence them as
much as they influence us. If we can stay out
of their poison, refuse to play, we can help to
clean up the atmosphere.

Our ordinary notions of politeness often lead
us to encourage emotional polluters. We may
not see that our tacit acceptance and cooperation harms both us and them. Let us use our
faith in our common nature to behave cleanly;
we will thereby help others to clean up their
acts.

I'll try not to confuse politeness with pollution.

> *If we seek to be loved—if we expect to be*
> *loved—this cannot be accomplished; we will*
> *be dependent and grasping, not genuinely*
> *loving.*
>
> —*M. Scott Peck, M.D.*

We receive love when we give love, with no strings attached. Bargaining for love is sure to disappoint us. It's human nature, when bargaining for anything, to hope to pay only half of what something is worth. Expressing this attitude in our relationships guarantees that we'll be shortchanged.

No one of us is free from the need for love. And most of us search for reassurances of that love from the significant people in our lives. However, the search will be unending until we come to love ourselves. Love of self is assured when we understand our worth, our actual necessity in the larger picture of the events that touch us all.

When we realize our value and see that life's mysteries have reasons, we'll no longer doubt ourselves and we'll be free to love and understand another's value too. We need never grasp for love when we sense the real meaning of the lives that surround us.

I will love someone fully today and I'll understand their meaning in my life.

The true wonder of the world is available everywhere, in the minutest parts of our bodies, in the vast expanses of the cosmos, and in the interconnectedness of these and all things.

—Michael Stark

Let's take a moment and look around ourselves. All that we see has its connection to us and to all other parts of this vast universe, and there is a universal rhythm with whose beat all life is in tune.

Our existence, all existence, is to be marvelled at. How perfect is the rosebud, the baby's toenails, the dog's sense of direction. We are not alive by accident. The beat of our hearts is necessary to the continued beat of the Universe. The whole is maintained by the combination of all the parts.

Life is sacred, all life. Friends and enemies are sacred. Lovers, children, parents are sacred. When we've come to understand this fact, understand it to the depths of our being, we'll know love; we'll know ourselves. Most of all we'll feel the peace that accompanies faith in the vastness and the rightness of the Universe and all it contains.

Everything as far as my eyes can see and heart can feel is contributing a part to my personal existence today.

*Imagine that we conjure up a world that is
safe for mothers and daughters.*
                                        —Louise Bernikow

The question of violence and danger in society
occupies a lot of time, breath, and printer's ink.
The possibilities of peace and safety take up very
little. It is usual for us to think of containing
violence by greater violence: the violence of
weapons, of prisons, of riot squads. And yet the
teachers whose wisdom we prize above all
others tell us that one cannot answer force with
force; that only peace and detachment can meet
violence and draw out its poisons.

No sane person wants war. Yet we are so
locked into violent patterns of thinking that
many of us believe we should prepare for it.
How would we go about preparing for peace?
What are the first steps we could take? What is
peace, anyhow? We seem to know very little
about it.

A world that is safe for mothers and daughters would be safe for fathers and sons as well.
Let us search our hearts to discover what we
know of peace, and let us talk to one another,
work together to realize our knowledge.

*I shall not study violence any more; instead, I shall dis-
cover as much as I can about peace and safety—for in my
life, peace begins with me.*

January 20

It is not fair to ask of others what you are not willing to do yourself.
—Eleanor Roosevelt

Equality is a state of mind. When we value our own self-worth, we are comfortable with the achievements and the well-being of our friends and associates. Criticizing others, making demands we don't want to fulfill ourselves, are symptoms of a punctured ego.

Most of us experience wavering self-confidence on occasion. It may haunt us when a big task faces us. Or it may visit us when we least expect it. It's a facet of the human condition to sometimes lack self-assurance. At times we need to remember that life is purposeful, and the events involving us are by design.

Almost daily we'll face situations we fear are more than we can handle, and we'll hope to pass the task off to another. It's well for us to remember that we're never given a task for which we're not prepared. Nor should we pass on to others those activities we need to experience personally if our growth is to be complete.

I must do my own growing today. If I ask others to do what I should do, I'll not fulfill my part of life's bargain.

Let me listen to me and not to them.
                        —*Gertrude Stein*

Our ears would fill with advice, if we listened to it: advertisers, evangelists, publishers, educators, all clamoring to market their products, try to get us to conform to their notions of what we should be.

One of the dangers of a democratic society is confusing the individual and the mass—using statistical data to define persons instead of trends. "Trendiness" is a way of avoiding individuality. To choose for ourselves means taking responsibility for our choices, saying, "I do this because I want to."

Each of us has an interior voice that knows what we want. We know—even if the knowledge sometimes causes us pain—that we're unique individuals, with goals, programs, and behaviors distinct from others'. Acknowledgment and enjoyment of our full humanity means owning our differences—listening to our own voices.

I am the expert on my own life. Today and every day let me be wise enough to consult myself.

January 22

All our resolves and decisions are made in a mood or frame of mind which is certain to change.

—Marcel Proust

When we are alert in the here and now we are constant collectors of new information. Consciously and subconsciously we sift through it and file it away—not to be forgotten, however. Our opinions, our attitudes, and our responses to life are influenced and expanded by those moments in which we absorbed new information, moments that in turn enhance our credibility as flexible, thoughtful decision-makers.

It is much easier to keep our minds closed and our attitudes and behavior rigid. Venturing into uncharted territories need never be risked. Each day becomes predictable and dull—in time, not really worth living.

Life's joys lie in adventure. We're promised adventure every moment of the day if we open our eyes to it. The currents that flow from the activities around us are charged with reasons for reformulated plans, new opinions, advanced enlightenment. That we're fully contributing members of the universe is evidenced in our flexibility when called for by changing situations.

I can change my mind today with pride, if new information calls for it.

No person could save another.
—Joyce Carol Oates

We encounter the experiences we need in our lives. It's sometimes hard to believe that when we're grappling with disappointment, anger, or loss. Yet everything that comes our way is material for our growth.

Many of us entertain a fantasy that some person can complete us. We don't believe that we're complete in ourselves. Only when we do will we become able to share in a life-enhancing partnership with another person. Only when we love ourselves can we love others realistically, instead of seeing them as fantasy figures, projections of our own desire.

No one can hurt us emotionally unless we allow the hurt. We're full partners in everything that we do, and taking responsibility for our actions and our desires is our first step toward being fully lovable.

The only one who can save me is me.

January 24

He has the right to criticize who has the heart to help.

—Abraham Lincoln

Our negative judgements of others very frequently inform us of our own shortcomings. In other words, what we dislike in others are often those things we hate about ourselves. Much better than criticizing another's abhorrent behavior is a decision to look inwardly at our own collection of traits and attitudes. Our desire to criticize, to pass judgement, offers an excellent mirror of who we truly are. And the image we see reflected can guide our movements toward becoming healthier, happy individuals.

We can feel a bit of gladness for what our negative reactions are able to teach us—but we must be willing to learn from them. How exciting to contemplate that every hateful moment actually is offering us a positive opportunity for change.

It's human to find fault, and we shouldn't be overcome with shame. However, we hinder our own personal growth every time we quickly criticize another rather than rejoicing that we've been given an additional opportunity to move closer to the person we're being called to become.

Today I'll look beyond others' faults and recognize my own.

Is there any stab as deep as wondering where and how much you failed those you loved?
—Florida Scott Maxwell

Treating our loved ones as we hope to be treated is our assurance against failing them. And if we listen to our inner voice, we'll never falter in our actions toward others. There is always a right behavior, a thoughtful response, a respectful posture.

Let us be mindful that we're sharing our experiences with others who need the talents we have to offer. It's not by coincidence but by design that we're given opportunities to treat those close at hand in some manner. We'd do well to let the choice be loving.

How we treat another invites like treatment. Actions from our heart will soften our own struggles. Also, spiteful, critical treatment of others will hamper our steps. We teach others how to treat us by our gestures and words.

The inner voice can be heard if I choose to listen. It will never guide me wrongly.

January 26

I came into this world, not chiefly to make this a good place to live in, but to live in it, be it good or bad.

—*H. D. Thoreau*

To live is to open ourselves to possibility, to rule out nothing. There is no way we can spare ourselves, or those we love, the pains of living, because they are inseparable from the joys. How grandiose we are when we think we can save the world.

All we can do—and it's quite a lot—is to live the best way we can, achieving a balance amid the forces that pull on us: pleasure, responsibility, power, love. If we can live so that we respond to all of them, rule out none of them and yet enslave ourselves to none, we will have the best the world can give.

One quality all great people seem to share is humor—the capacity to see our struggles and triumphs with detachment. Not that our life is unimportant, but that it's only a part of the huge web of life on this planet.

If we can keep our lives in balance, we won't get puffed up by any little triumph, or squashed by a defeat. We'll keep on with our lives, confident that we're doing our best.

Let me not forget—my chief business in life is living.

I feel we have picked each other from the crowd as fellow-travelers, for neither of us is to the other's personality the end-all and the be-all.

— *Joanna Field*

It's not mere chance that we gravitate toward those who become our friends. Nor is it only happenstance that we are piqued by others. We are, in fact, on a journey and have much to learn. From our friends and even more so from those not so friendly, we are destined to learn what our souls yearn for. The journey is the process of enlightenment for which we all have gathered. From one another we are receiving that which we're ready to learn. All of us students. Each of us a teacher.

How comforting to know that the pain of a particular experience, or the confusion over a set of circumstances, will become understandable with the passage of time. All experience plays its part. All of our acquaintances share destinies overlapping our own. There is security in knowing that our journeys are necessary and right for us.

I'll not discount the value of any person or any experience that circumstances offer today.

January 28

A truth that's told with bad intent
Beats all the lies you can invent.
                                    —William Blake

The quality of our relationships with others depends heavily on our motives. If we're trying to change our friends, to correct their behavior or to improve their lives, we'll insure a poor quality of friendship.

The only life we have power over is our own. Trying to fix other people isn't only futile, it's disrespectful. Chronic "fixers" are likely to attract people who seem to cry out for their services. Over time, the situation usually proves to be a set-up for frustration and anger.

Self-respect begins inside ourselves. Real consideration for others demands that we treat them with the same respect we'd like to receive.

There is no such thing as my telling someone something "for their own good."

January 29

*I come from nothing, but from where come
the undying thoughts I bear?*
— *Alice Meynell*

Nothing is new under the sun, except each day as it dawns. The thoughts that visit our brains have all been thought before; the freshest, brightest, best ideas and inventions all have their roots in ancient visions of human possibility.

Yet this day is new because it is our January 29. The elements that make it up may be immortal. They have not ever come together in just this way before. We feel at home in the timelessness of our spirits and the sense of the unique possibilities of today. We will be given many chances, today, to be the person we want to be.

We have no power over the events of today, except our power over our own behavior. If we act from our knowledge of what is right for us, all will be well.

I am unique, and I have inherited the rich medium of thought.

January 30

Maturity is the capacity to withstand ego-destroying experiences, and not lose one's perspective in the ego-building experiences.
—Robert K. Greenleaf

Our emotional health is proportionate to our willingness to take personal responsibility for thoughtful responses to the myriad circumstances in our lives. We are not powerless over our attitudes or over behaviors, even though we are generally powerless over the events themselves. The most troubling of times need not diminish us, unless we let them.

Likewise, the flavor of the most pleasurable situation retains its long life in proportion to our willingness to assimilate the experience gradually, letting it enrich us but not overwhelm us. Overreaction to any event casts a spell over us, inhibiting our ability to perceive accurately the moments, hours, perhaps even days of experiences that follow.

Finding the balance between overemotional reactions to people and circumstances and disinterested passivity takes effort and a commitment to emotional health. And that balance is the real key to experiencing a life that's joyful.

No event need throw me today. And yet, every situation offers me a chance to practice healthy living.

January 31

*It seems to me that in the long run it is im-
possible to maintain a democratic society
unless you can spread the benefits and burdens of being an American citizen reasonably
evenly.*

—*Felix Rohatyn*

In our relationships, in our work and play, do
we assume an equal share of the burdens, and do
we get a reasonable amount of benefits in exchange?

There's no way to calculate the burdens and
benefits of living. But our own inner awareness
is a pretty accurate measure: if you feel ripped
off and resentful, then something's wrong; if
you feel guilty, as though you were getting away
with murder, something's wrong.

Often we're reluctant to track down the
source of our guilt or our resentment; we're
afraid that what we find may force us to change
the way we live and work, and change is painful.

Letting go of a source of pain can be as difficult
as losing a source of pleasure.

*I am the only one who knows just what is going on in my
life, and all such choices are mine.*

February

*You are a child of the universe no less than
the trees and the stars; you have a right to
be here. And whether or not it is clear to you,
no doubt the universe is unfolding as it should.*
—Max Ehrmann

There is a patterned sequence to the events
surrounding us, attracting our attention, inviting our personal involvement. We must accept this as a given, and then attune ourselves
to the rhythm of the ordered flow. This will
augment our personal growth and facilitate our
contributions, which are both needed by other
players in this sequence of events.

We need not understand the full picture of
the pattern we're each woven into. We need
only trust that it's a design which will comfort
us—if not today, then tomorrow.

*I can go forth today—sure that events will move me in
the right direction even though I can't see what's around
the corner. There will be no unplanned event in the big
picture.*

February 2

*. . . we ourselves are only fragments of exist-
ence, and our lived life does not fill the whole
of our capacity to feel and to conceive.*
— Paul Valéry

Our feelings are bigger than we are. The love,
sorrow, fear or rage that any one of us feels at
any moment is just a thin slice of a great stream
of feeling that runs through all of humanity. To
experience strong emotions in a crowd, for instance, takes us out of ourselves.

Mob anger can be viciously destructive. Mob
joy can be transcendent. The difference between one individual and the mob is that each
one of us can choose, every moment, what we
will do with our emotions. We can feel rage and
choose to express it without harm. We can feel
sorrow and survive it. We can choose to dwell
with feelings that console and enhance our
spirits, and we can choose to let go of those that
diminish us.

With feelings, as with everything else, the law
of life is change. We shall not always feel as we
feel now. If we accept our feelings as they come,
and try to feel them fully as we're able, we shall
become more unified with our fellow human
creatures, and with all existence.

Pressure builds up behind a dam. I will let my feelings flow.

> . . . *fear makes strangers of people who should*
> *be friends.*
> —*Shirley McLaine*

Life is sterile and stifled when we close our-selves off from the smiles or swift glances of others. The opportunities we have for personal contacts are not mere chance. We draw to our-selves experiences and thus acquaintances which will lend meaning to our lives.

Our fear of others is generally tied to our sense of personal inadequacy. How frequent are our suspicions that others are smarter, more capable, destined for greater success. However, we fail to gain the growth promised by another's presence in our lives when we give in to the fears that haunt us all at times. Those strangers in our lives are not without purpose. Their growth, as well as our own, is dependent on the removal of the barriers separating us.

A stranger lingering in my life is not here by chance. I will gain from opening myself.

February 4

> *No one can make you feel inferior without your consent.*
>
> —*Eleanor Roosevelt*

Self-talk is powerful. It will develop a healthy ego. Likewise, it can trigger ego deterioration. Our strength in times of trouble can be doubled or eroded depending on the commitment we've made to positive self-worth.

A secure self-image and unwavering self-confidence are characteristics we all long for. They need not elude us; they are our birthright. However, most of us fail to understand we need only to claim them to own them. Instead, we doubt our abilities, question our self-worth, and discover that our strength and our potential are exactly what we think they are.

Belief in ourselves precedes achievement. Our successes are always within our power if we understand our responsibility for them. We are self-talking every moment; the words we use are our personal choice.

I'll be conscious today of my self-talk. My experiences will directly reflect my thoughts.

It's important to know that words don't move mountains. Work, exacting work moves mountains.

—*Danilo Dolci*

Exercising our spiritual muscles for the arduous and exacting work of faith is a new thing for many of us. Our culture doesn't seem to put the same value on spiritual power as it does on muscles or intellect. Yet a strong and agile spirit, the kind that can do the work that moves mountains, is possible for us all.

Like the muscles of our arms and legs, the spirit swells and grows with use. Small acts of faith will show us the way. As we grow increasingly secure, we are capable of greater and greater leaps of faith. Real prayer, real meditation, means touching and using that inner core of faith, and the more we do it, the stronger it grows.

The fullest life is possible for those whose powers are the best developed. If we choose to move mountains, we must be prepared to work. Even achieving freedom of choice in our lives means developing our spirits.

My spiritual power matches the task at hand. As I become stronger, I can accomplish greater things.

February 6

*In this world everything changes except good
deeds and bad deeds; these follow you as the
shadows follow the body.*

— *Ruth Benedict*

Our identity, our being at any moment, is a
composite of all we have been in the past. Some
of our actions have made us wiser. Others haunt
us because we didn't put forth our best effort.
All of our deeds contributed in some measure to
our growth, however, and they can guide our
choice to behave honorably today.

Acceptance of who we are, our total self, is
necessary for our emotional maturity. Shame
for past actions will keep us stuck. Our restitu-
tion for the past is best made by responsible behavior today. How fortunate that each waking
moment offers us opportunities to become our
better selves.

*Today, just like every day, I'll make choices to behave in
ways that will fill me with pride or shame. I pray for
thoughtfulness today.*

*With history piling up so fast, almost every
day is the anniversary of something awful.*
                                        —*Joe Brainard*

"History" is mostly a record of awful events—
war, famine, conspiracy, oppression, betrayal.
But surely, every day is equally the anniversary
of something wonderful. It's all in how you look
at it.

Perhaps a calendar of wonderful anniver-
saries would be an antidote to depression: this is
the day I first heard tender words from someone
dear; this is the day I stopped smoking; ten years
ago on this day I committed myself to a program
of positive living and spiritual growth.

Keeping such a calendar, even for a short
time, gives us a record of spiritual progress.
Even to be able to say, "How different I am from
what I was five years ago" can be a truly cheer-
ing thing. Why let the tyranny of history de-
press our spirits? Let's make our own.

*I will treasure the private record; the public one will keep
track of disasters.*

February 8

He who angers you, conquers you!
—Elizabeth Kenny

It's by choice that we let others control our emotions. When we make that choice we have abdicated our personal responsibility for growth. Deciding to feel how we truly want to feel rather than giving someone else control is freeing, exhilarating and nourishing.

When we let someone anger us, we have decided to make them the object of our attention, and any intention to do what needs to be done is gone. Anger consumes us. With it we become preoccupied and the growth and contributions we were created for come to a standstill. Our personal power to think creatively and to take action are lost when we choose anger instead. For this way, the object of our anger decides who we are.

Today I'll be in charge of my growth if I choose to determine my own emotions.

Imagine there's no country. It isn't hard to do.
Nothing to kill or die for. And no religion,
too.

—*John Lennon*

If we let go of all conventions of life as we know it—the laws, religions, customs and other institutions—we could train our imagination to build new ones, perhaps based on different values of work and wealth and play.

What is our image of an ideal society? Perhaps it is one in which there is no money. Or one where all work is done by computers and people are free to play. Perhaps our model is military or tribal.

How would we define crime or punishment in our Utopia? What would be the criteria for success and failure? Would we redefine the family as we know it? How would we reward our heroes? Whatever our ideal society is, it's likely to express our most deeply held values.

To find out what I hold most precious, I will try to imagine giving it up.

February 10

Limited expectations yield only limited results.
—Susan Laurson Willig

Our thoughts determine our actions, and when our thoughts are negative, our successes are few. What we hold in our mind is certain to be reflected in the day's activities. And we are capable of fueling our thoughts positively, if we choose to.

Positive self-assessment and uplifting pep talks can become habitual if our desire to live up to our potential is great enough. The expectations we privately harbor, be they small or far-reaching, will set the pace for the progress we make today, and every day.

We can greet a challenge with eager anticipation when we've grown accustomed to believing in our capability for success. First, we must expect to handle, with poise, whatever confronts us.

No one but me determines my course today. My success begins in my mind.

*SERVICE. A beautiful word fallen upon
bad days.*

—*Claude McKay*

Silver service; military service; tennis service;
evening service. The word has so many different
connotations that we lose the thread that con-
nects them; something done *for another*. Whether
it's our profession or our gift, service is our
offering of skill or care to a fellow being.

We now have the term self-service, which
mostly connotes convenience in shopping. Do
we ever truly serve ourselves, in the sense of
offering our best to our own benefit? A high
quality of self-service is an important part of
self-esteem. By taking time for ourselves, treating ourselves gently, we demonstrate our belief
that we deserve love.

Quality self-service doesn't only mean caring
for our bodies, although that's important. It also
means forgiving ourselves, letting mistakes
remain in the past, and nourishing our spirits
with good thoughts, good words, good deeds.
If we're to earn tranquility and joy in life, surely we can learn to serve ourselves with kindness.

*Today will abound with opportunities to serve myself
and others. I'll be open to them.*

> *For have you not perceived that imitations,*
> *whether of bodily gestures, tones of voice, or*
> *modes of thought, if they be persevered in from*
> *an early age, are apt to grow into habits and a*
> *second nature?*
>
> —*Plato*

What does it mean to act *"as if"*? When we feel angry and unforgiving, it means we act *as if* we forgave someone who stepped on our toes, or took our parking place, or ruined our paint-brush; when we feel cold and self-pitying, it means to act *as if* we were warmly interested in the child or friend or spouse who has something to tell us. It can be a wonderful exercise. If we really give ourselves to the performance, we can act *as if*, and the mood we imitate becomes real.

Oscars will never be given for acting *as if*, but the rewards are far more useful. Acting *as if* can salvage a bad day; it can repair or prevent a quarrel. Act as if we didn't have a headache, and often the headache disappears. Act as if we weren't in a hurry and often we will have time for everything.

When we were small, adults said to us, "Don't make a face or you'll freeze that way." Now that we're grown, we can learn how to imitate, flexibly, what we want. Instead of freezing into negative postures, we reach for agreeable ones—and so often *"as if"* becomes *"as is."*

Today I shall practice acting as if I were serene; perhaps it will grow into a habit.

*Every truth we see is one to give to the world,
not to keep to ourselves alone.*
—Elizabeth Cady Stanton

Sometimes we feel that we are the guardians of a fragile, threatened civilization: if it weren't for us, all would be lost. Such feelings are a signal that we need to check out our reality, to test our perceptions of the world against those of someone we trust. We are seldom in sole possession of the truth!

But shared commitment to truth is powerful; it enhances our spirits. Most of us feel a need to express this commitment, whether by sharing worship or simply talking with friends. Often the truth is a process, a relationship between ourselves and others, and sharing it gives it roundness and luster.

I need courage to face the truth; and the truth will strengthen me.

February 14

It is not the things we accomplish that are important, it is the very act of living that is truly important.

— Dr. Bill Jackson

We've been invited to participate in this life, to be present, one to another, and that's all that's expected of us. Our successes may bring us personal joy but our value as persons lies only in our being.

But living fully is more than just making an appearance, here—today. It's celebrating our oneness—our ties to one another—our need for one another's presence to complete our own. And we can be a celebrant only when we're involved and fully focused on the experience. We capture life's gifts, its riches, when we are intent on the moment's fullness. We miss what we most need when our hearts and minds are distracted.

All that's asked of me is rapt attention here, now, to others. And I'll find the good life.

*I had often occasion to notice the use that was
made of fragments and small opportunities in
Cranford . . . . Things that many would despise, and actions which it seemed scarcely
worthwhile to perform, were all attended
to. . . .*

—Elizabeth Gaskell

Our lives are full of "fragments and small opportunities." Bouquets of wild grasses, shells
and pebbles from the shore, a half-hour visit to
a convalescent home, small acts of kindness,
found poems—anything that enriches the moment, for ourselves or for another, is worth
performing.

And it's the busiest people who seem to have
time for these fragments, time to smell the flow-
ers. It's often a shock to realize that doing something nice for ourselves might involve a small
deliberate kindness to another. But the more we
are good to ourselves in this way, the richer our
lives become.

*The moment is mine to cherish and to share. When I share
a kindness, I double it.*

February 16

You can't cross a chasm in two steps.
—Rashi Fein

When a small child hides her eyes, she means, "You can't see me." We sophisticated grownups sometimes have trouble getting rid of magic thinking. We tear petals from daisies, one by one; we tell ourselves that anything we eat standing up has no calories. We know one must leap across a chasm, but still we think, "If only I could change feet in the middle!"

The important thing is getting to the other side—tackling the problem on its own terms. Playing magic games is one way to stay stuck. There's nothing romantic or admirable about futile efforts; they're an admission that we don't want to succeed.

Every problem teaches us how to resolve it. If we can't see the solution, then we're not ready for it, and instead of sputtering vainly we should set that question aside and address ourselves to our appropriate tasks.

I will remember that wishing almost never makes it so. Wishing and working almost always do.

*. . . concern should drive us into action and not
into depression.*
—*Karen Horney*

If a situation in our lives causes concern, be
it mild disgruntlement or serious frustration,
we should understand that our concern indicates that we need to act, responsibly. Events
that attract our attention need our action.

Our actions can take many forms. Occasionally we will be called upon to take charge of a situation. More often, offering emotional support
to another is all that's needed. Perhaps most
frequently, our prayers are enough.

There is always a proper response to any circumstance that causes us concern. If we choose
no response, our inaction will only heighten our
concern. And preoccupation will hinder the
day's activities.

*My actions today should reflect my concerns and be ap-
propriate to the need.*

February 18

If the only tool you have is a hammer, you tend to see every problem as a nail.
— *Abraham Maslow*

When we can take a long view of our problems, we can sometimes see that we're using inappropriate tools to try to solve them. What's necessary for us to do is to move away, to detach. That may show us a whole new context into which our problem fits—and in which it may not even be a problem.

Detachment is hard to achieve when we're deeply hooked into a situation. When we send ourselves drastic messages like "now or never!" we're pressing our noses right up against the problem—a position in which it's difficult to maintain a balanced view. To stop and say, "If not now, then perhaps some other time," unhooks us and lets us remember that life is richer and more varied than we thought when we were hooked.

Crisis thinking can be like a hammer—it flattens everything. This can be our way of trying to control the outcome of our individual struggle. But when we remember that we make up only small parts of one grand and beautiful design, we can surrender our problems to it.

To be a competent worker, I will seek out the tools that are best suited to my task.

Eyes, what are they? Colored glass,
Where reflections come and pass.
Open windows—by them sit
Beauty, Learning, Love, and Wit.
                    —Mary Elizabeth Coleridge

How we appear in others' eyes can become an obsession. Do they see me as I see myself? Or do they see the Real Me—and is that worse, or better? Are the eyes of others mirrors, in which I'll find only my own reflection? Or are they windows, through which I can touch the spirits of those I love?

We can never know the real lives of others, but we can trust that they are not so different from our own. The experiences we share are more powerful than those in which we differ; others struggle with the same temptations and surrender to the same destiny as we do.

If we esteem ourselves, we won't worry about others' opinions. Of course we want to be respected, loved by those we love, accepted as a fellow traveler on life's journey. But our main concern is our own spiritual growth—and it will be the key to how we are perceived.

Today, I'll look within and seek to please myself.

February 20

Do not dream of influencing other people . . .
Think of things in themselves.
　　　　　　　　　　　—Virginia Woolf

One sort of plan is doomed to almost certain failure: the plan we have for someone else. An experienced breeder can predict a pedigreed puppy's future with reasonable accuracy, but a human child is quite a different matter. Any relationship that is built on our expectations for another turns into a bitter struggle, a disappointment, or both.

There is one person, and only one, on whose life we can have a strong, positive influence, and that is each one of us. What's more, we deserve our own support. We'll richly repay our efforts in our own behalf. Anything we can do for ourselves will stay with us; the more we learn, the wiser we'll become.

"Things in themselves" are the actual things in our lives, now: our work, our play, our relationships, our spiritual growth. These things deserve our best efforts. As we become more and more the persons we want to be, we will discover the spheres we are meant to inhabit, and learn to welcome those who share them with us.

My efforts in my own behalf are never wasted.

*Although the act of nurturing another's spirit-
ual growth has the effect of nurturing one's
own, a major characteristic of genuine love is
that the distinction between oneself and the
other is always maintained and preserved.*
                              —M. Scott Peck, M.D.

Those we love must be free to love us in return, or leave us. The honest evidence of our
love is our commitment to encouraging another's full development. We are interdependent personalities who need one another's
presence in order to fulfill our destiny. And
yet, we are also separate individuals. We must
come to terms with our struggles alone.

One gift of life available to each of us is security, the sense that accompanies the recognition
of our spiritual center. Helping someone else
discover their spiritual gifts strengthens our
own. Nothing is too difficult when we act in
unison as separate entities, relying on the spiritual core that strengthens us to meet any situation.

*My own spiritual center will be strengthened if I help
someone else develop theirs.*

February 22

Happiness is the meaning and the purpose of life, the whole aim and end of human existence.

—*Aristotle*

We find happiness with our friends, if we expect it there. The workplace guarantees it too, if we go in search of it. Happiness visits us in our solitude and in our myriad involvements. Wherever we are, so is happiness, unless we've chosen to keep it out. Our attitudes are powerful, and will prevail in all matters, with all people.

Happiness is contagious. It spreads quickly when shared freely. When it catches up with us, the cares of the day are immediately lightened. We have lessons to learn in this life, and we have essential contributions to make, contributions that will ease another's burdens, foster happiness in another's heart. Likewise, someone else's lessons may well encourage our own happiness.

Every struggle is eased by laughter. I am never left to struggle alone, unless by choice. Today will be joyful and eventful if I live in the laughter.

When we think of cruelty, we must try to remember the stupidity, the envy, the frustration from which it has arisen.
— *Edith Sitwell*

Our outer behavior matches our inner state of mind and emotional well-being. Our expectations of others are consistent with our personal expectations. When we feel less than adequate because of our imperfections, we treat others like failures too. How someone treats us today indicates how that person feels about herself or himself.

Self-love is lacking wherever people criticize others destructively, and self-love is necessary before we can offer love to any of the people in our lives. Developing self-love requires discipline. Our existence verifies our value as human beings. Understanding that our lives do have purpose contributes to our ability to love ourselves.

Today is day one for me to develop my loving behavior.

February 24

*If you shut your door to all errors, truth will
be shut out.*

—*Rabindranath Tagore*

Since so much of the world remains mysterious, how can we rule out new possibilities? It's very human to want to cling to the little bits of truth we're sure of; but we mustn't use those bits of knowledge to keep us from the possibility of further discoveries.

True wisdom includes the humility to acknowledge what we don't know. The careful scientist and the experienced physician are humble before the immensity of what they don't know.

New experiences, new relations and connections can reveal more and more, if we are open to them. Once we decide we know something—and close our minds to the possibility that we don't—we're keeping ourselves willfully ignorant. Filtering out life's richness robs us of our birthright—experience. Nothing is true that can't stand to be tested against life's flow.

Even welcome visitors can only enter through a door I've opened.

*Relationships are only as alive as the people
engaging in them.*
                                        —Donald B. Ardell

We receive from every experience in proportion to what we give. In other words, the richness of our lives is necessarily dependent on the depth of our commitment. Reserved involvement guarantees only limited rewards, while whole-hearted efforts promise full-scale returns. In all aspects of our lives, we'll find this to be true.

Our relationships gift us justly. These experiences with others are woven together, and their beauty is equal to the beauty we bring to one another's company. However, if we bring only criticism and bleak hopelessness to a relationship, we'll find despair rather than joy. Every relationship is the sum and substance of the partners involved. No relationship is more fruitful than the efforts of those doing the pruning.

How much do I give to the relationships I deem meaningful? They bless me in just proportion to what I give. Today gives me a chance to make a greater contribution.

February 26

> *Self-determination does not mean exercising intellectual mastery at all times over bodily, earthly processes, though the capacity for that mastery expands our human possibilities.*
> —Linda Gordon

Growth means learning the limits of our will. What appears to be mastery—flying in an airplane, for example—is merely cooperation with natural forces. Human intellect does not *master* natural processes; we tap into them, learn them, bring our own aims into harmony with them.

The world is not a jungle, to be hacked, cleared, or bulldozed. Human beings are learning not to clear jungles that way either. The world is us extended over the globe. We can spend our whole lives discovering the wonderful oneness of creation.

The awareness of this unity expands our human possibility, for each case is an example of our growing harmony with nature.

I will pray for harmonious resolution of my human possibilities with the great forces of nature.

God creates. People rearrange.
                                    —Joseph Casey

Being alive is our invitation to act in fresh, inventive ways. All it takes is concentrating on our inner vision in combination with external reality. The components for accomplishing any task are at our fingertips, awaiting discovery.

Our burdens are lightened when we understand that all situations are resolvable—no mystery need leave us in the dark for long. Just as surely as we each exist, so exists every element we need to solve any problem or chart any new course. Our purpose in life is to select those elements that will satisfy the need. We each have been blessed with this capability for proper selection.

The day promises challenge and many choices. I can successfully handle all possibilities.

February 28

I want somehow to tell the story of how the dispossessed become possessed of their own history without losing sight, without forgetting the meaning or the nature of their journey.

—Sherley Anne Williams

To use the past without being controlled by it—that is our responsibility to history. Because the past is irrecoverably vanished, it's sometimes tempting to forget it or to falsify it. But being true to ourselves means being true to our history.

Past cruelties can remain powerful in our lives—yet to take possession of our history means to free ourselves of bondage to past events. Nothing can ever change them. If we are to make the future good, we'll learn what the past can teach us. But our freedom requires us to make choices based on the needs of the present, not the past.

I can act at every moment in such a way as to honor the past and enhance the future.

*Patience is a particular requirement. With-
out it you can destroy in an hour what it might
take you weeks to repair.*
                              —Charlie W. Shedd

Enjoying the moment, in its fullest, makes
possible a peaceful and patient pace. Progress is
guaranteed if our minds are centered, in the
present, on the only event deserving of our
attention. We can be certain that error and
frustration will haunt us if our attentions are
divided.

Patience will see us through a troubled time,
but how much easier it is to savor patience when
it's accompanied by faith. We can know and fully
trust that all is well—that our lives are on course
—that individual experiences are exactly what
we need at this moment. However, faith makes
the knowing easier and the softness of the
patient heart eases us through the times of challenge and uncertainty.

*Patience slows me down long enough to notice another,
and to be grateful for the gifts of the moment. Patience
promises me the power to move forward with purpose.
Today's fruits will be in proportion to my patience.*

March

*It is time to show the strength of water and
flow away. . . . To stand is to be crushed,
but to flow out is to gather new strength.*
—*Marge Piercy*

Water is one of the strongest elements on
earth: it can't be broken; it can assume many
shapes; it joins easily with itself. When it reaches
a certain mass, moving water presents an irre-
sistible force.

We might do well to learn to acquire the
strength of water temporarily; to be able to
lose ourselves for a time, in concert with others, and then to reclaim our identities. We
needn't fear their loss. We are unique person-
alties, and our selfhood is intact.

*How successful I would be if I could use the strength of
water when I need it; the purity of air, the solidity of
earth, and the appetite of fire.*

March 2

One's mind may be given readily and it may be given with zest. Not all control is oppression. Sometimes it is release.
—Gilbert Ryle

Our most dangerous delusion is that we can control others. The hard-won truth is that we can control only ourselves—and it may take us a lifetime to learn this. Self-control means release, however; release from the bondage of uncontrolled and thoughtless behavior. When we recognize that our only legitimate power is over ourselves, we become free to grow spiritually and to increase that power.

Lack of control is not freedom; it is chaos. Conflicting impulses squander energies instead of controlling them and directing them toward growth. We can't subdue our unruly selves by fighting them: accept them, love them as part of our human imperfection, our superb and jagged individuality.

As we come to recognize the benefits of self-control, we'll choose it more and more often. We'll become more fully in control of our lives, better able to direct our energies and do what we want to do.

Only by choosing self-control will I achieve freedom.

*Love is mutually feeding each other, not one
living on another like a ghoul.*
—Bessie Head

Real love is compromise. It's sharing and
taking turns. It's putting someone else's best
interests first. Love wears many expressions
and is demonstrated by many gestures. Offering love to someone, when the offer is genuine, benefits the giver as much as the receiver.
Our calloused souls are softened by the gentle
nature of our love. No one of us develops men-
tally and emotionally to our full stature if we
cultivate isolation rather than intimacy.

We learn who we are through our involvement with others. We come to terms with our
defects and have opportunities to enhance our
assets while experiencing the strengths and
shortcomings of others. What time and patience
teach is that love is generally slow to develop
but will result when there is a mutual decision
to live and grow in one another's company. Each
person we genuinely love makes our own survival easier.

*My love is best expressed when I help someone else live
life more comfortably.*

March 4

The art of pleasing consists in being pleased.
                    —William Hazlitt

Others' pleasure in our company becomes our pleasure. If we can set aside our self-conscious anxieties and simply enjoy being with others, they will enjoy us. As lovers know, there is no aphrodisiac like a loved one's desire.

When we give one another our full attention, we enhance one another's humanity. Much of life consists of routine transactions, in which people hardly recognize each other as human. Even intimate relationships can come to suffer if we withhold ourselves.

When we discover pleasure in each other's company, we kindle a spark of joy that illuminates far more than the moment.

Today I will decide to be fully human in all my encounters.

. . . you don't get to choose how you're going to die, or when. You can only decide how you're going to live. Now.

—Joan Baez

The responsibility we each are charged with for our individual development is awesome, particularly when we look ahead to our whole life stretching before us. It's not uncommon to be immobilized with the fear of making a wrong decision, heading down a dead-end path. It's with great relief that we realize that the tomorrows will take care of themselves if today is well lived.

Lives well lived, a hope that's cherished by us all, are not beyond our simple grasp. Attention to the demands of the moment only, coupled with the decision to behave in ways that will fill us with pride, will insure that our experiences are generally smooth. The attitude we carry into any situation will influence the outcome, our growth, but most of all the quality of our whole lives.

I need to concern myself with today, only. And live it well.

March 6

"Freedom ain't nothing but knowing how to say what's up in your head."
—*Ralph Ellison*

The freedom to speak our minds is a precious gift. Throughout the world, throughout history, it has been and is a rare privilege. The privilege should oblige us in return to broaden and strengthen our minds, so that what we speak is worthy of free people.

The obligation is not to be perfect; the search for truth proceeds by trial and error. It is to be generous, forgiving, and honest. A moment's thought before we speak might save us and those around us many petty words.

We can't choose our feelings. From time to time we'll be swept by feelings that we wouldn't choose. But we can choose our actions, and speech is one. We can always choose to speak or not. Often it's wiser not to speak out of negative feelings. If we remind ourselves that free speech was a hard-won right, we may have more respect for the way we enjoy it.

A moment's reflection may keep me from abusing my rights—or others'.

Nothing happens to any man that he is not formed by nature to bear.
—Marcus Aurelius Antoninus

Reflecting on the past reveals that indeed we do find the strength and the ability to cope with whatever experiences ripple our calm. Moreover, we have come to accept that the tides of turmoil wash in new awarenesses, heightened perceptions, measurable calm.

Tragedies are guaranteed to trigger first pain, then perceptible growth, and finally, tranquility. Over and over again we pass through these stages that are designed to nurture our fuller development as healthy human beings. Over and over we see that the tough times teach us what we're ready to learn.

We can look to the day ahead fully expecting to be strengthened enough to handle whatever we've been readied to experience. Nothing will present itself that can't be coped with.

Today I can be certain of growing. I will meet the challenges in unison with my inner strength.

March 8

*". . . you never get over bein' a child long's
you have a mother to go to."*
—Sarah Orne Jewett

For most of us, our mothers were the first love, and the quality of our relationships throughout life is influenced by that earliest one. A mark of real maturity is the ability to see our mothers simply as human beings—lovable, fallible, interesting, and imperfect, just like ourselves.

Some of us have suffered a mother's early death; some of us cope bravely with her long illness. Few of us have a simple, easy relationship with our mothers. Too much is at stake. The infant that needs its mother's arms lives on within us all.

Few of us have such a continuous bond with our mothers, but we're fortunate if we can have an adult relationship that includes the love and nurturing we crave, because we never get past the need for it. The most successful intimacy seems to be based on reciprocal nurturing, for we need to give as well as to receive.

The child I was lives within me, and so does the mothering caretaker I first loved.

*All great reforms require one to dare a lot
to win a little.*
                                —*William L. O'Neill*

Unfortunately, life does not come with a money-back guarantee. Going after what we want, especially if we're up against established interests, is likely to demand the commitment of our best energies—with no certainty of getting it.

Oddly enough, some of the happiest people we are ever likely to meet are those who devote their lives to seemingly hopeless causes. For such people, daring a lot can mean staking their lives on a belief. The outcomes are bound to be small in proportion: failure, perhaps. At best, limited achievement.

But none of this seems to matter. In fact, a happy person with a cause seems to have totally let go of the outcome. The joy is in the struggle, in the process. They learn so much; and by living for something outside themselves, their own small problems miraculously fall into line.

Today I'll keep in mind that achievement is risky, but dedication wonderfully liberating.

March 10

One cannot have wisdom without living life.
—Dorothy McCall

Understanding circumstances, other people, even ourselves comes with the passage of time and our willingness to be open to all the lessons contained within a moment. We must be willing to participate fully in the events that have requested our attendance. Then we can discover the longed-for clarity about life and our role in it. Immersion in the moment accompanied by reflective quiet times promises a perspective that offers us wisdom.

We all long for happiness, an easier life, and wisdom. We learn so slowly that both happiness and the easier life are generally matters of attitude. Therein lies our sought-after wisdom. How much simpler it makes living through even our most feared experiences when we have acquired the wisdom to know that the mind we carry into the moment, any moment, will be reflected in the outcome.

It takes patience and willingness to live fully enough to reap the benefits that accompany wisdom.

Today I'll practice patience.

*What most of us want is to be heard, to com-
municate.*

—*Dory Previn*

The need to know that we count in the lives
of others, that our presence has not gone unnoticed, is universal. Few of us are blessed from
birth with full knowledge of our connectedness
to all life. Instead, we falter and fumble our way
through our experiences, uncertain of our
worth and meaning. Acceptance by others is our
want. Unconditional love is our due.

Since we all share this same need to be acknowledged, it's best we each offer acknowledgment to those sharing our experiences today.
They aren't unlike us; their needs and insecurities match our own. We'd all survive the
harsh bumps of life with so much greater ease
if we felt the comfort of others. In the company of others nothing is too much for any one
of us to handle.

*Today I'll remember that others need my comfort and
willingness to listen just as much as I need theirs.*

March 12

There are two tragedies in life. One is not to get your heart's desire. The other is to get it.
—George Bernard Shaw

Desire is strong; we all feel it. Desire can impel us toward positive, life-enhancing experiences, or it can fasten on vain and unproductive ends. Material things will never satisfy desire; only a serene spirit and a detachment from outcomes will enable us to live peaceably beside the torrent that is our desire.

In itself, desire is neither good nor bad. How we direct our desire, and whether we join it to our love or to our anger, determines the effect it will have in our lives.

If our desire is continually unfulfilled, perhaps we should examine, deeply and honestly, the direction we've allowed it to take. If achieving our desire leaves us feeling hollow, we should do the same. Desire can nourish us if we understand it as a continuous process, a part of our spiritual growth.

Let me be sure that what I desire is worthy of my best self.

The best thing for you, my children, is to serve God from your heart, without false-hood or shame, not giving out to people that you are one thing while, God forbid, in your heart you are another.
— *Glückel of Hameln*

We pray for wholeness of the spirit: to be able to live cleanly, with no shame, and to meet every aspect of life with the same serene face. It isn't easy for most of us. We fuss. We trip ourselves up. We may find ourselves telling lies, creating emotional turmoil to escape what we see as even greater turmoil.

The first step toward wholeness is for us to admit that we are human. No, not perfect; yes, about as flawed as everybody else. Once the knowledge is part of us that we're part of suffering, seeking humanity, a lot of falsehood and turmoil shears away.

There isn't any big secret to protect; there's just you, just me. However different we may appear, we're more than kin. And we can keep each other honest. The habit of honesty, once formed, is harder to break than the habit of lying.

I shall resolve to show the same face everywhere, and I'll become serene.

March 14

> *My children weary me. I can only see them as*
> *defective adults . . .*
>
> —*Evelyn Waugh*

If we expect children to behave as adults, of course we shall find them tiresome. If we expect water to be milk, we will be continually disappointed. But—since we can control and direct our expectations—why should we set ourselves up for such inevitable annoyances?

But we do. We are constantly expecting things unreasonably, and then being disappointed, shocked, heartbroken and betrayed. It would be so much more rational simply to take things as they come, without expectations.

But that would involve a degree of detachment that most of us would find impossible— even repulsive. It would mean unhooking our feelings from other people's behavior. "But I *care* about her," we say. "Of course I want her to . . . ." It doesn't much matter what we want her to do; get married, get divorced, brush her teeth at night, or come in before midnight.

What matters is our involvement, our expectations. We can care about her and still not feel hurt by her actions that may not be what *we* want. Hurtful actions are another matter; but she has a right to be who she is, just as we all do.

My expectations today will be only for myself.

*Gold, for the instant, lost its luster in his
eyes, for there were countless treasures of the
heart which it could never purchase.*
                                        —*Charles Dickens*

The mysterious thing about "treasures of
the heart" is that they are "countless"—bound-
less, self-renewing, inexhaustible. When we
love and are loved, trust and are trusted, this
reciprocal relationship gives us and those who
love and trust us a literally endless wealth.

Only when the relationship is one-sided do
we feel drained by our commitments. Love that
is based on mutual understanding and respect
will never drain us of our resources; our fund
of love is replenished even as it flows out of
us, as though the act of loving generates more
love.

Fear can impede this miraculous process. In
general, we have to know ourselves pretty well,
and be quite secure in our own skins, before
we can make to someone else the glad and unconditional gift of ourselves. Love entails
risk—the risk of being completely open, and
completely self-forgetful. But all success involves risk; and in this case the rewards are the
greatest possible.

I will not let fear keep me from the treasures of the heart.

March 16

> *Within our dreams and aspirations we find our opportunities.*
> —Sue Atchley Ebaugh

Our dreams invite us to broaden our horizons to reach beyond our present goals. They are much more than whims. They are probably calling us to those opportunities for which our talents have been readied. Most of us need this encouragement to attempt new ventures.

We've each been invited to this present moment by design. Our lives are joined like the tiles of a mosaic; none of us contributes the whole of the picture but each of us is necessary for its completion. More importantly, the depth, the richness of the picture in its entirety, is enhanced by our fulfilled dreams.

With joy and excitement we can anticipate our frequent aspirations, recognizing them as the guideposts offering directions for our daily travels.

Today I will welcome my dreams. They indicate tomorrow's successful ventures.

*Every outlook, desirable or undesirable,
remains possible for anyone, no matter what
his present outlook is.*
                              —Dr. George Weinberg

The attitude with which we greet the day,
approach a situation, or respond to a friend or
co-worker is fully within our control. We exercise absolute control over little in our lives, but
our attitudes represent personal choice each
moment.
   Recognizing the power inherent in personal
choice is exhilarating. It means we are free
from domination by others, if such is our choice.
Freedom to act, to think, to dream our own
dreams is ours when we exercise it.

*I celebrate my power today. I am free to choose my every
response to each encounter. Hallelujah!*

March 18

> *Life is curious when it is reduced to its essentials.*
>
> —*Jean Rhys*

Life is always reduced to its essentials. We're frail creatures: without water and shelter, we can't survive. We may not think of our lives in these minimalist terms, but accidents of many kinds can disrupt our fragile web of protection.

It makes sense, then, to assure ourselves of the best quality of life while we have it. This does not mean luxury or plenty; a high quality of life accompanies a high standard of behavior and relationships.

Clarity and honesty in our dealings with others will assure the quality of our lives. Simplicity is more satisfying than complexity. The less we get in our own way, the more clearly we can see these elegant essentials of life—elegant in that they are never extraneous. Life is indeed curious in the way it engages our full attention.

Like a curious child, life presents me with the most interesting questions. I'll be patient, and the answers will come.

We are apt to call barbarous whatever departs widely from our own taste and apprehension. But soon find the epithet of reproach retorted on us.
—*David Hume*

Judging others is a hazardous game that's likely to backfire. Labeling others is a form of judgment. It's a way of sticking people into pigeonholes and saving ourselves the effort of thought. Do we really want to be thoughtlessly tossed by others into some category not of our choosing?

The world's rich texture holds much that each of us will love, and much to which we'll be indifferent. How much more pleasant it is to look for—and to find—what we like, than to sneer at and judge what we don't. A need to judge others is a sign that we lack confidence in our own taste—an indication of shaky self-esteem.

Our personal growth asks us to look positively at life. We want to find occasions for rejoicing, not disapproving. The thoughtless and intolerant teach others that they themselves are not worthy of respect.

I will set aside my judgment of others and concentrate instead on freeing myself.

March 20

. . . you must remember that an arbitrary power is like most other things which are very hard, very liable to be broken.
—Abigail Adams

Sway is built into tall buildings so they won't break. Rigid structures are never as strong as flexible ones. The strongest minds are also the most nimble, the most ready to change and to include new information.

We only see one little slice of reality. How can we know what's right for others? Our spirits will be strong to the extent that we can keep them flexible, ready to incorporate new energies and to make fresh associations.

To be flexible doesn't mean to be wishy-washy or indecisive; often people who refuse to grow will say they want to "remain flexible." But one can be flexible and still have strong direction, generosity, and broad tolerance for others' growth. What cannot bend may break.

I'll respect the truth of your living, growing spirit. Your reality can be your gift to me.

*If our species does destroy itself, it will be
a death in the cradle—a case of infant mortality.*

—*Jonathan Schell*

Compared to rocks or to termites or ginkgo trees, our whole species is a very recent passenger on this Spaceship Earth. We've had a busy time of it, for the few thousand years that there have been enough of us to make a difference. But in time as geologists measure it, we have barely entered the history of the planet.

If we eradicated ourselves with the lethal means at our disposal, we wouldn't be the first species to disappear. But wouldn't it be a shame? We humans have the capacity for transcendence as well as destruction. Surely we're adaptable enough to guide our own development away from our current preoccupation with deadly toys.

Written history gives us just a tiny glimpse of life on earth. Let's live so as to guarantee that human existence lasts out its full chapter.

I am one of the earth's children. I will treat my parent with respect.

March 22

It is good to have an end to journey towards;
but it is the journey that matters, in the end.
                              —Ursala K. LeGuin

Our goals lend direction to our lives. Without them we flounder, often uncertain of who we are. They provide substance for our self-definition and they motivate us, at times even deeply exhilarate us. Nevertheless, it's the many steps, the myriad activities, the unexpected barriers along the daily journey that give real meaning to our lives. We are so much more than our completed achievements, and the process is what develops the person within.

It's far too easy for most of us to miss the moment and its richness because our sights are on a particular journey's end. How often do we fail to appreciate the many occasions for feeling satisfaction over a task well done? We seldom grasp the full joy of living because our sights are glued to the future.

It is a hard but easily forgotten lesson that a goal completed is always followed by a letdown. The joy resides in the process.

Can I stay with the moment and the activity before me, just for today?

*When I trust and respect myself enough to
be myself honestly, others respond with trust
and respect.*

—*John Stevens*

We can greet all situations today with ease if
we have committed ourselves to lives of integrity. Having made the decision to be fully honest
at all times eliminates our uncertainty in responding to others, and thus we don't cloud
issues and confuse our contemporaries with
inconsistencies.

Without fail we recognize others' integrity
as ours is recognized. It goes without saying that
each of us is more at ease with those we trust.

Honesty invites honesty. Self-respect encourages respectful behavior toward others, and
like a boomerang, it returns to the initiator.
We teach others how to treat us. With every
action we take, every word we speak, we are
informing others of our personhood.

*I will set the tone for my day by my behavior toward
self and others. Over this I am all-powerful.*

March 24

Being human is itself difficult, and therefore all kinds of settlements (except dream cities) have problems.

—Jane Jacobs

A sure cure for rage at the minor irritations of daily life is to sit back from the traffic jam, the broken appointment, the lost vital information, and say, "Being human is itself difficult." It may not cure our frustrations for long, but it's worth practicing.

Many of our troubles stem from forgetting just how difficult it is. We often have impossibly high standards for behavior, especially our own. We are complicated, marvelous creatures who have many skills, but we thwart our own capacity for enjoyment by expecting that we will be perfect.

Being human is difficult; we perform it imperfectly. And when we combine our effort with others'—building a building, performing a play—we multiply our imperfections as well as our skills. Yet we need each other.

If we can detach ourselves from anger and disappointment and reflect on how wonderful it is that we can do anything at all, we may remember to love ourselves and others for our human complexity and simplicity.

Nobody's perfect; such is the nature of my humanity.

> *. . . we will be victorious if we have not for-*
> *gotten how to learn.*
> —*Rosa Luxemburg*

There is no goal beyond our grasp, no achievement beyond our attainment if we reduce our
natural barriers against new information and
new perspectives. Our victories accompany
perseverance, fearless learning, openness to
the unfamiliar.

Each of us is experiencing a particular period,
with a select group of people, by design, not by
chance. Myriad situations call us, and messages
secure our attention because they contribute
to our potential for victory. What's asked of us
is rapt attention to the moment, intense openness to its richness, and a willingness to be
edified or humored or perhaps simply nurtured.
We will gain from every moment's offering
whatever we need for our continued growth and
ultimate victory.

Learning is forever in my control. The decision is per-
sonal, and perhaps must be made each day, anew. The
choice is mine.

March 26

When you have become willing to hide nothing, you will not only be willing to enter into communion but will also understand peace and joy.

—*Anonymous*

Keeping secrets is synonymous with keeping stuck. Our human potential is stifled by our stuffed feelings, attitudes, ideas. Conversely, the more we allow others to really know us, the greater will be our opportunities for growth and happiness. Our secrets burden us.

The choice to shield our inner selves from others is ours to make. Risking vulnerability takes strength, and a great deal of courage. We can never be certain that our audience won't betray us. However, we can be certain that words and thoughts hidden will haunt us.

The gift of total honesty and openness is profound intimacy. It's this gift that makes possible a level of friendship that dispels self-doubts, that gives rise to a euphoria that turns all situations into opportunities for greater happiness.

I may be tempted to keep some secrets today. I will remember that sharing them will relieve me of a burden that weighs me down.

. . . we do not always like what is good for us in this world.
— *Eleanor Roosevelt*

Today will call each of us to make our particular contributions to the moment. There is no guarantee that we will enjoy every experience, but we can be certain each one of them will teach us something we're ready to learn because "when the student is ready, the teacher appears."

Little reflection is necessary for us to realize that our most troubling times have generally been responsible for our greatest growth. Our achievements are always accompanied by periods of frustration, occasional loss of direction, even momentary despair because the actual results miss the mark of our hopes. However, the passage of time makes clear that these actual results benefit us far more than those we'd hoped for.

Our personal vision is narrow and limiting. We can't really imagine what's in store for us. The most we can do is trust that our experiences have our best interests in tow.

I'll remember: Today I'm a student and my experiences are my teachers.

March 28

> *The person who fears to try is thus enslaved.*
> —Leonard E. Read

Immobilization is fear's result. In its grip we fail to move forward. We fail to think new thoughts, live new experiences, chance new personalities. All that life is prepared to offer us goes ungreeted.

Let us remember, we have been given the gift of life and we are obliged to test our wings and spring forth, displaying the message that's within. Even when fear crouches close at our heels, we can elude its grasp if we remember this message that eternally accompanies us: "All is well."

Life is a series of opportunities for emotional, spiritual, and intellectual growth. No opportunity for action is beyond our capabilities.

I will look to this day only. I will be invited to participate in those experiences designed for my particular development. All is well.

*A house is no home unless it contains food
and fire for the mind as well as for the body.*
—*Margaret Fuller*

No matter how full our social and professional
lives are, we all need a base, a place where we
are at home. Whether it's a studio apartment
furnished from second-hand stores and garage
sales or a luxurious country retreat, one of our
basic human urges is the need to make a home.
And our spiritual fulfillment asks that our
home nourish us.

Look around: in our choices for our home,
we reveal what nourishes and inspires us. Perhaps we opt for the comfortable and well-used:
old books, chairs that speak more to the back
and bottom than to the eye. Perhaps we are
restless and change the way our homes look
frequently. We all use our homes to express
our desires.

Are we neglecting "food and fire for the
mind"? Sometimes we misinterpret inertia as
comfort. Are we giving our minds a wholesome
environment?

*Fuel for my spirit is never wholly consumed. Today, I will
look to my supply.*

March 30

If you can imagine it, you can achieve it.
If you can dream it, you can become it.
                            —William Arthur Ward

Our dreams and our aspirations are our invitations to set new goals, attempt new tasks, dare to travel uncharted courses. We each have gifts to offer our fellow-travelers, but most frequently need encouragement to recognize our own strengths and talents.

Seldom do we rise in the morning fully eager to join in the opportunities that await us. More likely we have to prepare our minds, center our emotional selves, nurture the inner person who may fear the experiences the day promises.

It's normal—completely human— to be conscious of our incompetencies while lacking awareness of our abilities. To them we give scant attention, generally blocking out the praise they elicit. To our failings, however small, we compulsively devote our attentive minds. We forget that today's abilities were last year's incompetencies.

Achievements today will be many, and they are indications of past dreams. My hopes today guide me toward future achievements. My failings are few and help to keep me on track.

*Freedom is like taking a bath—you have
to keep doing it every day!*
— Flo Kennedy

Nothing stands still. Change is the law of life.
We may sometimes feel that our personal gains
have to be won over and over again. But, looked
at from another perspective, that's not so: our
solid personal gains are the ones that no one and
nothing can take away from us.

They are tools for continued growth. Jobs,
lovers, houses may change, but serenity and
freedom of spirit are within our power to
achieve—to maintain—or to give away.

Freedom means choice; our choice of what
we do with our bodies, our money, our lives. If
we decline to choose, the choice will be made for
us. If we don't use or claim our freedom, we are
giving it away. Our lives need our active, creative participation every moment.

*Like bathing, I must daily exercise my freedom. No one
can do it for me.*

April

In the transformation and growth of all things, every bud and feature has its proper form.

—Fritjof Capra

Our lives are a series of unfoldings. Our struggle to be perfect at every stage of life is a common element of the human condition. What comes with age and wisdom is acceptance of our imperfections. We see that we develop at every stage of life.

We can rejoice that we're unfolding according to the needs of our existence. Each day is ushering in new growth, subtle changes. Our transformation is lifelong and according to specifications known to the inner self—our connection to Universal Wisdom.

The changes we'll experience today are compatible with the new growth we adapted to yesterday. And likewise, what will come next week, next year will have been prepared for by the tiny transformations accumulated on this road to maturity. We are developing exactly as we need to each step of the way. And our fit, yours and mine, one with another, is perfect at every moment.

I am changing, growing, maturing at every moment— according to plan.

April 2

We must assist natural processes that serve the function of reunification.
— Joseph G. Hancock

Some families in mild climates have begun to experiment with unified living: recycling wastes, growing food, and using only renewable sources like the sun and the wind for power. Seen from the twelfth floor of an apartment building, in sub-zero weather, this is a radical gesture. Yet it's a conservative way of living, asking for little, spoiling nothing, and putting back into the earth everything that's taken out.

We can all put back what we take out, but are we as careful of our emotional and spiritual processes? Or do we sometimes block them or try to erase them or hoard them up? The universe is one sphere. Energy flows through it, through polar bears and bacteria and Republicans and cranberries. Surrendering to the flow is our only way of achieving personal reunification.

I can assist natural processes by giving my assent, freely choosing unity.

*Time is a dressmaker specializing in altera-
tions.*
                                    —Faith Baldwin

We are learning as we go, and the experiences
shed light on our own plans for proceeding.
The steps we are taking, in unison as well as
on separate but parallel paths, enhance the
particular movements of us all.

We often expect perfection from ourselves,
forgetting that we're all beginners in life. The
best we can do is willingly acknowledge our
errors, grateful that we can always begin again
on any task—grateful that we have the experiences of others to help guide us.

Life is process. We learn, we grow, share
burdens, reformulate ideas, and restructure
our values. Every change we make alters the
steps we take, altering in turn someone else's
movements, too.

*Today I'll discover a change I need to make, one that will
reach further than my own task.*

April 4

He was the victim of his own rage . . .
—Paule Marshall

Our negative behavior always turns on us. So does our positive behavior. Obviously, it's better to have joy and peace rebound on us than violence. Then why don't we consistently act peaceful and joyous?

It probably takes an idiot or a saint to be consistently positive in this world of cynicism, cruelty, and corruption. However we may strive to free ourselves of preoccupation with things beyond our control, we all find ourselves reacting to certain events with rage, envy, fear, or other painful, destructive emotions. But knowing we have a choice can free us from bondage to this pain.

We can choose to respond ragefully or enviously—or we can choose to feel the feeling and then to let it go, so that the negative feeling doesn't control our behavior. Successful living involves learning to control how we behave; if we hide or deny our feelings, they're with us forever. It's only by letting them go that we can be truly free. And it's only by experiencing them that we can let them go.

I can only spread joy if I stop being a victim of my own despair.

April 5

If you would be loved, love and be lovable.
—Benjamin Franklin

We all desire to be loved. Our common human characteristic is our need to count in someone else's life. At least one other person needs us, we tell ourselves, when we feel least able to accept life's demands. How alike we all are. The paradox is that our own need for love is lessened when we bestow it on others. Give it away and it returns. A promise, one we can trust.

The reality about love and its path from sender to receiver and back again is often distant from our minds. More often we stew and become obsessed with the lack of love's evidence in our lives. Why isn't he smiling? Why didn't she care? Has someone more interesting taken our place? Choosing to offer love, rather than look for it, will influence every experience we have. Life will feel gentler, and the rewards will be many and far-reaching.

Loving others promises me the love I desire. But I can't expect it if I don't give it first.

April 6

> . . . (I)t was not so much that they drifted,
> as that in the presence of a boat the world
> drifted, forgot. The dreamed-about changed
> places with the dreamer.
>
> —Eudora Welty

Dreams can be so potent and mysterious that many of us, at one time or another, have felt that they put us in touch with some other level of reality. Sometimes we wonder if we're dreaming our waking lives, too. Some of us have had the fantasy that we're characters in someone else's dream, or in some great world-dream.

Sometimes our dreams show us what we want; or what we fear. Dreams are like messages sent from one part of us to another: scrambled messages in which the people, places, and happenings from many epochs of our lives come together.

Sometimes we may dream a great happiness, or a wonderful solution to a problem. Such dreams cast a rosy glow over our whole day; as a nightmare can make us feel uneasy for a long time. Such dreams may be messages about feelings we're not feeling. The dreamed-about —fear or joy—does seem to change places with the dreamers, who have shut the feeling out of their waking lives.

Owning our dreams, cherishing them, is part of fully accepting ourselves. However silly, scary, sexy, or confusing a dream may be, it is our dream, we made it.

I don't need to crack the code to get the message.

*Speak kindly today; when tomorrow comes
you will be in practice.*
                              —Anonymous

Behavior is habitual: we thoughtlessly brush
our teeth, set our alarm clock, start our car,
or dress in order. We create rituals in our lives,
and they free us from thousands of small decisions, leaving our minds less cluttered for the
more important choices. However, every action
we choose sets into motion a behavior that may
become habit. We should be wary of habits that
harm ourselves or others.

We have the personal power, with every
decision, to choose to act in ways that promote
well-being—our own and others. For instance,
a tense situation might be better served by a
smile and a deep breath than a harsh response.
Knowledge of our freedom to choose such a
response exhilarates us. We should be mindful
that every response that is frequently made is
approaching habit, and our habits determine
the ease with which we greet and adapt to the
conditions life offers.

*I am a creature of habit. The power is mine to create
positive habits. I will make careful choices today.*

April 8

*I refuse to pronounce the names of possession
and nonpossession.*
                                    —*Monique Wittig*

New relationships require new names. If we
want to stop behaving in a customary way—as
an adversary, as a victim, as a bully, as a mar-
tyr—then we need new words to describe our
new behavior.

Perhaps we glimpse the possibility of a new
relationship to power—that one might use
power, yet not subjugate others. Perhaps we
glimpse the possibility of sharing, of lateral extensions rather than hierarchies.

It's clear that if we are to change the world,
we must begin by changing our relations with
others. Perhaps we don't want such a grand
project as changing the world, but we might
want to change old ways of using our skills.
Let us be fearless and trust in the knowledge
of our hearts.

*The only way I can discover the consequences of change
is to change.*

Make yourself necessary to someone.
   —Ralph Waldo Emerson

We are each positioned, not by chance but by design, within the context of home, job, friends, and acquaintances. Our involvement with life around us, the myriad experiences that confront us, guide our growth. The gift of life obligates us to contribute our best efforts, our talents to the situations involving us. From them we'll gain exactly those lessons we are ready to handle.

Creation is interdependent. Every element, every human, every organism is necessary to the completion of the whole. How comforting to know that our existence is not mere chance. The space we take here, now, is advancing the development of all aspects of life. We never need to doubt our value, our importance to others. Being alive is the ultimate proof that each of us is necessary to the many persons in our lives. Gratitude for them, and for us, will strengthen our understanding.

I will look upon my many human contacts today with real understanding. I am here by design.

April 10

*If an idea, I reasoned, were really a valuable
one, there must be some way of realizing it.*
    —Elizabeth Blackwell

These words were written by the first woman
who earned a medical degree. They're useful
to anyone who fears that their most precious
dreams are doomed to failure.

If our dreams are valuable ideas, they will be
useful goals. If they're childish fantasies, they
won't, although those can be fun. It's important
to distinguish the ones we can achieve from the
ones we can't. The first kind will nourish us,
like bread; the others, like candy, won't.

We have a responsibility to those nourishing
dreams, because they come from what's best
in us. Our responsibility is to live so that the
dream might be realized. When dreams become
goals, they have a way of calling us forth. Goals
organize our lives, so that we may reach them.

*Reaching my goal is never as important as the progress
I make toward it.*

April 11

Happiness is not a matter of events; it depends upon the tides of the mind.
—Alice Meynell

It's all too easy to blame a friend, spouse, or co-worker for the uneven quality of our lives. If only others would behave according to our plans and dictates, then all would go well, we think. What seldom is remembered or even understood is that each of us has an individual perspective on any single event—our own. We need to stretch our minds and hearts to understand an experience from another's point of view. However, we need never fully understand how another perceives life. We need only to accept that another's perspective is legitimate.

Our happiness is not dependent on the perceptions or the actions of someone else. Nor is it dependent on attention, or lack of it, from a loved one. Our occupation may be challenging and fulfilling; however, the joy we get from it depends on the attitude we carry to the job. In every way, whether in the company of others or by ourselves, we make our own happiness.

My opportunity for happiness is guaranteed if I opt for it today.

April 12

We must be true inside, true to ourselves,
before we can know a truth that is outside us.
　　　　　　　　　　　—Thomas Merton

Integrity is not a given in everyone's life. It is the result of self-discipline, inner trust, and a decision to be relentlessly honest in our response to all situations in our lives. We are quick to recognize this quality in others, and hope to acquire it ourselves. However, we must cultivate risktaking and cast off fears of rejection and derision if we're to discover the serenity a fully integral life offers.

Recognition of truth in others, realization of the appropriateness of decisions or the aptness of choices is made easier when we're certain of the truth of our own lives. The inner turmoil dissipates and we are quiet within when we choose to live lives full of truth. And in the quiet we discern all truths. How much softer the edges of experience when we're guided by truth. How much easier every decision, every choice, when we've committed ourselves to a course of total honesty.

My level of peace is my responsibility. I will find just as much as I need.

You can have your cake and eat it. But my
God, it will go rotten inside you.
                              —*D.H. Lawrence*

When we try to hang on to another person or to any part of life, we impede the natural flow. To be in harmony, we must let go. "You must lose your life in order to find it." Real strength, real self-respect is achieved only by setting the hungry self aside.

It's human to want to hold on to what's precious. But life's real treasure is found in achieving the rhythm of ebb and flow. Joy can't be a constant state. Glory is part of a cycle that includes defeat.

Accepting imperfection, accepting change, is part of accepting our humanity. We obey the same cyclic laws that govern the universe. Success in living depends on accepting that one day we'll eat cake and the next we won't. Fear tempts us to hoard the crumbs of our success, but wisdom lets us brush them away.

I will remember that joys recur just as sorrows do.

April 14

We must build human relevance into the
paradigms of science itself.
            —Steven Rose and Hilary Rose

Science itself is not to be feared. We fear what
science is capable of—just as we fear what human beings are capable of, when they act on
their violent feelings, without control or choice.
Science is a powerful tool of the human mind,
when it's used with respect and tenderness
for the unity of life.

It isn't human relevance we need so much as
relevance to this seamless unity. As our capacity
for knowledge grows, we glimpse more clearly
how interrelated all human efforts are with the
great rhythmic processes of the planet. The
paradigms of science are the models it makes of
the world. When scientists make a model that
ignores relevance, they risk using their knowledge stupidly, or harmfully.

We need to recognize that science is part of
our human endeavor—not more nor less than
art or agriculture or raising children, but part
of all of them (as they're all part of science). We
must remember how broad a definition of human relevance we need, when we contemplate
the unbroken beauty of the world.

There is a choice in all activity; so I will prepare to choose
well.

Promises that you make to yourself are often like the Japanese plum tree—they bear no fruit.

—Frances Marion

Promises are merely empty words if they aren't backed up by action. And action is generally preceded first by deliberate resolve, then verbalized commitment (often to someone besides ourselves), and finally, a carefully laid out plan of steps to be taken. Promises that are made, but not kept, quickly hamper any progress we dream of making. They hang like weights on our shoulders, reminding us of our weak resolve.

Only actions can fulfill our promises. Perhaps we'd do well to make a promise, any promise, only for a day. We can always renew it tomorrow.

The additional and unexpected gift is that a promise kept, no matter its magnitude, enhances our self-image. And since we can only live one day at a time, no promise need be made for longer. All of us can manage to fulfill one promise, for one day, if we believe in it and in ourselves.

Today offers me the opportunity I need to feel better about myself.

April 16

I am ashamed of these tears. And yet
At the extreme of my misfortune
I am ashamed not to shed them.

—*Euripides*

Shame is a little whip we always carry with us. We can shame ourselves easily; the little whip stings. We often use it to punish our feelings, because they evoke the helpless children we were. So we learn to suppress our feelings of fear, or rage, or desire. We would rather not feel at all, than feel the sting of shame.

Why should we punish our feelings? Everyone feels much the same things. Why should our humanity shame us? Perhaps somewhere we acquired the notion that it's wrong to be human; that an inhuman perfection is the only proper public image.

Love can heal the pain of shame. Self-love and self-acceptance can make us strong enough to discard the little whip. We're much more lovable when we acknowledge our humanity and let go of our shame. We're also better able to love others. Shame shuts us up; love opens us to joy.

I'm grateful for my feelings; they're close to my capacity for love.

*Noble deeds and hot baths are the best cures
for depression.*
                                    —Dodie Smith

Preoccupation with ourselves exaggerates whatever condition presently haunts us. The temptation to dwell on our pain is so great, it takes strength and a serious commitment to emotional health to move our focus to another's needs. We are slow to learn that our own pain is soothed each time we offer comfort to another in pain.

Periods of depression will foster compassionate thoughtfulness, if we're willing to take advantage of the natural inertia that accompanies the blues. Our moments of stillness give us time to take note of another's condition. And it's through consideration for another that our wounds are cleansed and healed.

Rarely do we offer rapt attention and sincere concern to the troubled individuals in our lives. And yet, each one traveling our same or parallel pathway needs the attention that only we can give. Our own spirit is nourished every time we offer love to someone else.

Well-being, my own and someone else's, will be fostered by my actions today.

April 18

> . . . [F]atherly and motherly hearts often
> beat warm and wise in the breasts of bache-
> lor uncles and maiden aunts; and it is my
> private opinion that these worthy creatures
> are a beautiful provision of nature for the
> cherishing of other people's children.
> —Louisa Mae Alcott

Nature has beautifully provided that all humans can love all other humans. We don't have
to be related by blood, nationality, or even language. Unlike the great apes, we have no un-
breakable patterns of rivalry and aggression;
we're free to choose love as our means of relat-
ing to the world.

Many people choose a sort of great-ape behavior, instead of enjoying the miraculous freedom of their power to cherish others. The choice
of mistrust, rivalry, and aggression sometimes
threatens to imprison us all in a zoo, surrounded
by fences and patrolled by guards.

The choice is ours: can we leave the apes
behind? Human love looks risky, from a cage.
Let's dare to be human today.

I can choose to bestow the gift of my love.

The edge of the world does not look far away,
To that I am on my way running.
                    —*Papago Indian song*
                    for a young girl

All things seem possible to us when we're
young. The world's problems look solvable; our
optimism and our immense youthful energy
combine to make us hopeful and impatient.
Why didn't anyone see it before? It's all so simple: if people would just love each other. . . .

As we grow older, we learn more about the
complicated system the world is. We learn that
everything is interrelated, and that none of our
simple youthful solutions even addressed the
problems. In fact, we learn that they aren't
problems, they're how the present system is
working. If we want to change those features
that we thought of as problems, then we have
to be prepared for everything to change.

If we're wise, we also know how to keep that
rapture; how to rekindle the belief that all is
possible. Not because we believe in our power
to change the whole world, but because the
vision is beautiful, and gives us the energy.

*The end may be in sight, but today's journey is all I
really have. Let me make the most of it.*

April 20

Every great mistake has a halfway moment,
a split second when it can be recalled and
perhaps remedied.
　　　　　　　　　　　　　　—*Pearl S. Buck*

We make mistakes because we are human, we are imperfect, we are frequently out of touch with the rhythms of the moment. When our minds are one place, either still trapped by the past or in limbo due to fear of the future, we fail to revere the experience of the present. And only when we salute completely the moment do we respond accurately to its meaning.

Seldom is a mistake as important as we allow it to be. Always we can rechart our steps; never is a task completed without some modifications along the way. Perhaps we'd do well to consider all mistakes as simply modifications in the original plans. Corrections triggered by mistakes may well be responsible for better outcomes. In fact, mistakes may be part of the process necessary to keep our spiritual program focused. Their role in our lives may be of greater significance than we'd ever imagined. However, we shouldn't dwell on the mistake but, rather, on the remedy.

Today I'll have to modify my steps, probably a few times.
And that's to be expected.

Courage is fear that has said its prayers.
—Anonymous

No one of us is always courageous. With trepidation we embark on many journeys. Fear is dispelled each time we rely on our inner strength and trust that our lives are in good hands.

Self-talk is powerful and will prepare us to meet whatever lies ahead today. Self-talk is like prayer and quiets our fears, making it possible to give our full attention to the events transpiring. Self-talk, when positive, cultivates a healthy self-image, one that offers security, even in the face of disaster. We all carry on a dialogue with ourselves much of the time. Taking charge of the messages—making sure they enhance our personal well-being, is an option always available to us.

No situation is more than we can handle. Whatever courage or strength is needed is as close as our willingness to go within, to commune with ourselves.

I must own my fears before I can let them go. Courage follows closely on their departing footsteps.

April 22

She walks around all day
quietly, but underneath it
she's electric
angry energy inside a passive form.
The common woman is as common
as a thunderstorm.

—Judy Grahn

Many people spend their days in anger and aren't aware of it. The conditions of work and life make many of us angry; we feel powerless to change them, and our frustration angers us more.

The Serenity Prayer asks for "the serenity to accept the things I cannot change; the courage to change the things I can, and the wisdom to know the difference." If we examine our lives fearlessly, we may find many things that are in our power to change.

Since we cannot change, or do not choose to change some things, we'd do well to accept them, instead of spinning our wheels in unproductive anger or turning the anger in, against ourselves. And when we summon the courage to change the things we can, our lives will bless us.

Today I'll look at anger as something I've chosen, instead of something inevitable. Is it covering fear? How can I resolve it?

*One often learns more from ten days of
agony than from ten years of contentment.*
                                    —Merle Shain

Pain pushes us, sometimes gently, sometimes
forcefully. It pushes us to make or accept
changes in our lives. We do not always welcome
change. Often the change even seems to inten-
sify the pain for a spell. But, in time we'll clearly
see the need for the change.

The peaceful periods in our lives have their
purpose, too. They give us time to rest, to grow
accustomed to the changes, to nurture the
"new self" that the changes made.

Accepting all experiences as necessary to our
development removes the negativity we are
likely to attach to these experiences. We might
instead choose to celebrate those difficult times,
recognizing their worth to our human potential.

*A positive attitude today will enhance the value of every
experience. The choice is open to me.*

April 24

I have learned silence from the talkative; tolerance from the intolerant and kindness from the unkind. I should not be ungrateful to those teachers.

—*Kahlil Gibran*

Every situation we experience, every individual we encounter offers us valuable insights about living life more fully. We learn what we appreciate in people by confronting what disturbs us. We are certain to learn more about ourselves when we acknowledge that which displeases us in the experiences that enjoy our attention.

It's all too easy to label "of no value" experiences that, on the surface, bore us. We also discount persons whose life experiences are different than our own. It takes a decision followed by concentrated effort to recognize the value of every moment. Each one is serving us a lesson that deserves our full attention, and it's frequently true that the lessons most helpful are the ones least appreciated or understood in the present.

I can be certain that whatever situations disturb me today are also guaranteed to offer me unexpected growth.

> [*In the 16th century*] *one has only to con-*
> *sider the difficulties involved in feeding a*
> *baby if the mother's milk ran dry.*
> > —*Philippe Airès*

Scientific progress has brought our society to the point where such a natural disaster as a milkless mother need have no consequences for her or her infant. Clean water, sewage disposal, immunization, and a widely available varied diet ensures relatively good health for millions. Sometimes this tempts us to look at the past as if it were another planet or the history of another species.

People had the same feelings four hundred years ago as we have today. Life was brutally hard; no families expected that all the children born would survive to maturity; people were old at 35 and often dead at 45. But they loved, feared, raged, and sought spiritual peace as we do.

Visiting old cemeteries is a moving experience, and an exercise for the imagination. Here is a man who buried three wives; here a family that lost four children in four years. We can reconstruct a different world in an hour or two and give ourselves an occasion for gratitude.

Imagining myself into the difficulties of the past can broaden my sympathies for the present.

April 26

It is more profitable to turn away thine eyes from such things as displease thee than to be a slave to contention.
—*Thomas À Kempis*

Focusing our attention incessantly on matters that disturb us, keeps us disturbed. And our obsession with our problems leaves no room for their solutions. However, we are only powerless in the face of difficulties if we choose to be. We are always free to search for the good which is lost in a tangled situation. We can be certain that our progress in life is equal to our capacity to let go of our problems and move ahead with the momentum of a positive attitude.

All too frequently, we fail to recognize opportunities for growth and success because we have chosen to be trapped by circumstances that are beyond our control. We may not realize this, but we are never tied to problems. Solutions are always within our grasp. However, we must let go long enough to gain a responsible perspective on the situation.

Problems need not stifle my growth today.

*All the strong things of her heart came out
in her body, that had been so tireless in serving generous emotions.*

—*Willa Cather*

We're always fascinated by beauty, and we
see it as the outward sign of goodness. For
young children, anything that brings pleasure
is good: soft fur, music, colored lights, candy.
What a disappointment to find that the soft
kitten has claws that scratch!

As we mature, our notions of beauty and
pleasure deepen and become more complex.
We see that beauty in people often is a reflection of their spiritual selves—and that physical
beauty is a little shallow and unsatisfying unless a generous spirit accompanies it.

That's what we call straightening out our
priorities: deciding or discovering that virtue
isn't boring, it's essential. Honesty, depend-
ability, and trust are what we look for in others
and what we strive for in ourselves. They wear
better than clothes or cars.

There's a saying, "In middle age, we have the
faces we deserve." Everyone has seen the wreck-
age that selfishness or dissipation can leave
on the faces of old beauties. When we have
strong, durable, compassionate spirits, we will
be good to look at.

*Strength and tenderness are more beautiful than high
cheekbones or curling hair, and I deserve them in my
relationships.*

April 28

A soft answer turneth away wrath but grievous words stir up anger.

—*Proverbs*

Our treatment of others in the home, at work, or play is our invitation for similar treatment. In fact, our every action, be it overt or covert, is noted by someone. We are always teaching someone how to treat us.

Anger is a seductive teacher. Unwanted tension, missed opportunities, stifled growth are all we can expect if we're trapped by anger. Our chances for creative fulfillment will be unnoticed when our attention is sapped by anger. But we can change our basic response to life. All it takes is a decision.

Just as powerful as negative behavior is a positive, friendly approach to situations and persons. We can decide to love life. And we'll find that smiles invite smiles. Respect generates respect. A serene attitude lessens tension in others. Each of us is responsible for our own actions and we each have the power to positively influence all experiences we share with others.

How I'm treated today will mirror how I'm treating others. Will I be proud?

*I too am born and
grown to be this thing only;
to be Anna in the world.*
          —Anna Rydstedt-Dannstedt

In all the world there is no one like you or like me. Even identical twins are not wholly alike. The sum of genetic information, experience, learning, desire, and memory that makes up each individual is absolutely unique. At any given moment we represent that sum—and the next moment the sum is different.

It follows that each of us is best in the world at one thing—being ourselves. To let go of competition with others is to release within ourselves the creative energy to be the best we can. We need never stop growing; the task of developing our individuality lasts our whole life. Fortunately, it's an absorbing task, and one that each one of us happens to be uniquely suited for.

To be ourselves in the world is a glorious thing. We should stretch our spirits so that we inhabit our lives fully, and we will learn all we can.

Let this day be my teacher, and my mirror.

April 30

In nature there are neither rewards or pun-
ishments—there are consequences.
                              —Robert G. Ingersoll

In life, as in nature, we experience the consequences of our actions. Some consequences
benefit us in very positive ways. Others teach
harsh lessons. But no action avoids having some
effect on our lives and on the lives of other
people, too. It is fortunate that each of us has
personal power over our actions. Individually
and collectively we are in control, every moment, of the actions that culminate in good or
bad consequences for all humanity.

It is easy to overlook the ramifications of our
haughty attitude toward a co-worker, or our
temper tantrum because we thought a loved
one let us down. We easily justify our treatment of others, and seldom take responsibility
for the consequences we triggered. And yet our
emotional maturity and our personal happiness is directly related to our commitment to
behave in a responsible manner. We not only
adversely affect others by our negative behavior, we hamper our personal progress, too.

My actions are far-reaching, as are their consequences.
I will take care to make them positive today.

May

*The body repeats the landscape. They are
the source of each other and create each other.*
—Meridel Le Sueur

The beautiful correspondences that structure
the world—from the five-pointed star in the
core of the apple to the snail-shell spiral of our
inner ear—can be a source of great comfort to
us. When we feel most alone, most abandoned
and out of sorts, the simple forms of beauty can
remind our eyes of the world's unity, and our
place within it.

Our path through the world is a part of it. We
add our individual voices to the chord that is
language, that is history. No matter how desperate we may feel, or how hopeless our lives
may seem at times, the fact remains that loss
and sorrow are a part of life, and the law of life
is change. Unless we choose to cling to sorrow,
it will flow through us. The next wave of feeling may bring us joy.

The hexagonal cells of the honeycomb recall
the shapes of insects' eyes, snowflakes, geo-
desic domes. We fit into this grand design.
We're here for a reason—for many reasons.
Let us treat ourselves as gently as we try to
treat the other parts of the delicate web of life.

*I stand in a reciprocal relationship with the world, part of
it as it is part of me.*

May 2

Resolve to be thyself and know that he who
finds himself loses his misery.
—Matthew Arnold

How confusing the issues in our lives can be when we try to accommodate all the views of the persons in our midst, persons who share few opinions in common. Agreeing with first one and then another is dizzying, and makes us suspect in the eyes of others. "Who is she really?" "What does he honestly believe?" We quickly become ill at ease in the company of those whose opinions we share only when it's convenient to do so.

We can be at peace when we've thoughtfully determined a course of action, and a world view that's compatible. Our attitudes, our opinions, and thus our responses to the currents of life will be consistent. When we develop integrity and strive to maintain it, rather than being in constant internal conflict because of our fluctuation, we discover a smoother passage over the bumps each of us can expect in life.

Today will be much less stressful if my actions reflect my inner self.

Our doubts are traitors,
And make us lose the good we oft might win
By fearing to attempt.
                              —William Shakespeare

Our own doubts are our greatest barriers in any endeavors. We are only free and able to accomplish what we think we can. When doubt arises, defeat is not far behind. However, that principle is just as strong in reverse. When we believe in ourselves, nothing can hold us back. Our accomplishments are many when we've developed the habit of self-assurance.

We must take personal responsibility for our beliefs, whether they be positive or negative. No one else is capable of putting thoughts in our minds. We have chosen those that are there. Far better that we coach our minds along positive paths. Only they can lead to the accomplishments which will give us satisfaction, today and every day.

We can anticipate our victories with excitement in this life. They will reflect what we've coached ourselves to attempt.

What I feel myself today will very much influence my achievement.

May 4

The most prophetic utterances have ema-
nated from the most poetical minds.
                    —William F.R. Stanley

What we call poetry is a capacity to use language so freely, so beautifully, and with so much
imagination that it transforms ordinary words.
What we call prophecy is the ability to see
through the complex machinery of the present
into the true nature of events. Both the poet
and the prophet seem to be touched with magic—with more than human powers.

They tear aside the veil of ordinary reality.
Both reveal a vision more intense than ours.
Yet we can learn from poets and prophets, if
we wish. Their vision is available to us.

All we need is humility and a willingness to
let our minds play freely. Great prophets and
poets speak to our human condition. Their
vision can challenge or console us, if we consult
them.

Truth is truth; I can recognize it where I find it.

He that knew all that learning ever writ
Knew only this—that he knew nothing yet.
                                        —Aphra Behn

It's true that the more information we have about the world, the more clearly we see the shape of what we don't know. It's also true that we don't need to learn anything at all in order to deal fairly with others and to walk gently in the world.

The wisdom that we need is inside us. Before our schooling teaches us to forget it, we know instinctively how to treat others because we know how we wish others to treat us, and we know that all people are one.

This primitive knowledge mustn't be buried under the classifications and analyses we pick up along the way. We can, if we try, de-school ourselves to the point where we can listen to our spirits, trust our bodies, and revere the world for the seamless whole it is.

If I cherish my original wisdom, then learning can help me to be comfortable in my ignorance.

May 6

Fear is only an illusion. It is the illusion that creates the feeling of separateness—the false sense of isolation that exists only in your imagination.

—Jeraldine Saunders

We are only alone in our minds. In reality, we are each contributing and necessary parts offering completion to the wholeness of the universe. Our very existence guarantees our equality, which, when fully understood, eases our fears. We have no reason to fear one another's presence, or to fear new situations when we realize that all of us are on equal footing. No one's talents are of greater value than our own, and each of us is talented in ways exactly appropriate to our circumstances.

Freedom from fear is a decision we can choose to make at any time. We can simply give it up and replace it with our understanding of equality with all persons. Taking responsibility for our fear, or our freedom from it, is the first step to a perspective promising healthier emotional development.

If I am fearful today it's because I've forgotten the reality of my existence. I am equal to all the people in my world, and we are necessary to one another.

There is no cardinal who does not aspire to the papacy.

—Stendhal

When we think of it, there is something truly remarkable in the fact that practically all human beings want to be better than they are. What a hopeful reading of the human race—four billion people, all eager to improve themselves!

For many of the humans on earth, self-improvement has an economic basis—to be able to eat two or three times each day, perhaps, rather than once. We are fortunate to be able to understand improvement in a moral and spiritual sense. Increased income or possessions cannot truly augment us; our real growth is inward.

However we understand our spiritual selves, most of us agree on how to foster them: through peace, silence, and beauty, in meditation, and in what some of us call prayer. Just as every bud aspires to be a flower, and as the flower holds the secret of the fruit, so we enfold the beauty of our spirits. If we nourish the spirit, we can grow to be our better selves. If we allow nothing to hamper its growth, our spirit will unfold.

I shall set my eyes on the clear path toward my spiritual unfolding.

May 8

Our true age can be determined by the ways
in which we allow ourselves to play.
                                    —Louis Walsh

Too few of us laugh as heartily as we might. We often fail to see the humorous side of our lives. We respond gravely to most situations, certain that a serious perspective is called for. We are unaware, it seems, that we're charged only with living responsibly. Never are we asked to be solely serious.

Any situation is easier to handle if our response is light-hearted. Laughter and playfulness ease the tensions inherent in certain circumstances. Taking life less seriously doesn't mean living less responsibly. Rather, it means freeing ourselves from the negative forces that may well encumber the circumstances facing us presently.

It's difficult even to recall what tripped me last week, and this fact alone should bring relief while I'm looking at today's potential hazards.

*Breaking through the foreground which is
the Playboys' Playground means letting
out the bunnies, the bitches, the beavers, the
squirrels, the chicks, the pussycats, the cows,
the nags, the foxy ladies, the old bats and
biddies, so that they can at last begin nam-
ing themselves.*

—Mary Daly

Racial and sexual stereotyping, casual put-
downs that consign another person to non-
human status, are so demeaning that it's hard
to believe the speaker really means them. We've
become so habituated to the putdown that it's
hard to be aware of how disrespectful this can
be, to ourselves as well as others.

This competitive attitude keeps us jockeying
for position, leads us constantly to measure
where we stand, and assumes that there's only
a limited amount of rightness in the world.

We're both all right, and if we're going to have
a relationship that lets us be self-respectful
as well as respectful of one another, we'll act
as if we're both all right. We won't call one
another chicks, pigs, big apes, or foxes. We won't
call each other by our body parts or our ethnic
groups, either; we'll recognize each other's
full and individual humanity.

*I will live today in honor of my name, and thus honor
others.*

May 10

*There are as many ways to live and grow as
there are people. Our own ways are the only
ways that should matter to us.*
> —Evelyn Mandel

Letting other people grow, develop, live their
own experiences as they must takes courage
and acceptance of the knowledge that our responsibility in this life is to our own healthy
development—not to controlling someone
else's.

It's not easy to let go of someone with whom
we want to share a particular path in life; however, no two of us are destined for exactly the
same lessons today, or any day. We must each
find our own way and develop those opportunities we meet that are certain to enhance
the lessons our souls have been created for.

Our need to control someone else generally
results from our own insecurities about life's
meaning. Because we lack understanding of our
own personal worth, we look for it in someone
else's devotion to us—a devotion that, in time,
we squeeze the life from.

We cannot control another's behavior, and
yet we try. And the more we try, the greater
the barriers between us become. Trust is all
we finally have that each of us is progressing,
according to our own pace, in rightful company.
We cannot force what is not meant to be.

*My own pace and direction is all that I need to be con-
cerned with today.*

The distance doesn't matter; only the first step is difficult.

—Mme. du Deffand

Life continually presents us with opportunities for achieving what we desire. "Only the first step is difficult." Each time we sense the possibility of a new direction in our lives, we are being given a chance to grow.

Sometimes the first step is a big one; sometimes we start to take it almost without noticing: a dream, a book, a conversation. Sometimes growth may come from *not* taking what looks like an opportunity. Whatever choice we make, we can be challenged to grow.

"The distance doesn't matter." Our road has many branching paths. What we work and pray for is the ability to see those paths clearly, and the strength to take a difficult first step.

Today my first step may be surrender.

May 12

Hope is a good breakfast, but it is a bad supper.

—Francis Bacon

Each day we hope for accomplishment and satisfaction, and we'll achieve these when we scale our hopes to our real capacities. There's no more satisfying feeling than finishing a project we've set up ourselves, tailored to our abilities, and worked at with patience and care. Our lives can be filled with such successes.

Learning to live means learning to keep ourselves in the present. This day is all we really have to work with. Of course, today will be influenced by what has already happened; and its influence will extend to tomorrow, next week, and beyond. But all we can make or do lies here, within this window of space and time.

May my supper be contentment. I'll breakfast on hope again tomorrow.

*To keep your character intact you cannot
stoop to filthy acts. It makes it easier to stoop
the next time.*
                                    —Katherine Hepburn

Good habits are as easily formed as bad ones.
It's quite likely that most of our daily activities
are routine. With little need for forethought,
we make our necessary motions every day. And
if we've behaved toward others in disrespectful ways on many occasions, we may thoughtlessly repeat those acts today.

Yet we should be grateful that we are in full
control of all actions we choose to take. No one
else has power over our behavior. No one else
can push us into actions for which we'll feel
shame or remorse.

Responsibility for who we are, in all respects,
is our birthright. Perhaps we don't always rejoice over this fact. And yet, it is the one absolute that guarantees we each have the power
to become who we wish to become.

*I'm creating behavior patterns today. Will they make
me proud?*

May 14

*However much we guard against it, we tend
to shape ourselves in the image others have
of us.*

—Eric Hoffer

Our sense of how someone else perceives
us is a compelling influence in our lives. At such
times we've often chosen not to rely on our
personal power, which can forge the posture
we want to present to others. We must put
forth the effort, however. Passively letting
others decide who we are gives us who we deserve!

We are not powerless in any situation. It's
true that we cannot control others, but the
reverse is likewise true. Unfortunately, too
often we let another individual decide our
worth, our capabilities, our very personality.
Domineering parents may have done it in the
past. A hateful boss or a too-critical spouse
may do it presently. We are always responsible
for our participation in someone else's under-
estimation of us. We are who we want to be.
The question we must answer is, why do we
choose to satisfy someone's negative image?

*Self-talk will help me maintain the self-image I choose
today. I will accept personal responsibility.*

*A man is rich in proportion to the number
of things he can afford to let alone.*
—H. D. Thoreau

Conscious, careful selection of those activities, situations, or people to whom we'll devote attention is all that separates centered, serene people from harried men and women. All of us are bombarded by myriad requests for some form of personal involvement. The temptation is great to attend to first one thing and then another, passively and superficially. However, our lives are enriched only when we commit ourselves to a deeper level of involvement, and to the few, rather than the many.

The talent given each of us shines forth if it's been nurtured, coddled, encouraged. We must become immersed enough in a project or an experience to lose self-conscious reservations if we're to discover the real weight of our talent. We know ourselves fully only when we're able to let the talent within define the posture without.

I can't be all things to all people today if I'm to be the person I need to be, for me.

May 16

*I am determined to maintain the perpen-
dicular position.*

—Lucy Stone

Perpendicular lines make right angles; they
make possible extensions of both height and
breadth. Right angles are weight-bearing. We
speak of asserting something "squarely," making perpendiculars.

People who speak their minds freely and
assert their individuality feel perpendicular;
the corners they create, by their points of view,
are sturdy and open. Others can use them to
build structures on.

It's important to claim the perpendicular,
even though we may feel pressured into curved
or parallel positions. If we're centered in ourselves, others won't throw us off balance. Each
of us needs to find our own center so that we
can occupy our own place. Others will recognize us. Together we'll build high and wide.

*My remotest ancestors dared to point their spines up-
right. I'll carry on the project they began.*

Who cannot give good counsel? 'Tis cheap,
it costs them nothing.
—*Robert Burton*

Other people's problems are so easy to solve.
Isn't it amazing how much better we are at their
lives than our own? Of course, other people's
lives don't hook us emotionally, by means of
love or guilt or precious delusions. We can look
at them wisely, with detachment.

Detachment is the key to solving our own
problems too, except that the detached intelligence may see a solution we're unwilling to
use—especially if it means changing our behavior. Then we may feel despair. We're stuck,
between the rock of our intelligence and the
hard place of our reluctance to change.

Whether we stay stuck depends on us. We can
choose to live as hybrids, a little wise, a little
infantile; a little happy, a little miserable. Or
we can risk change and growth. Within us is
the knowledge and power to get what we want,
if we'll believe in ourselves.

My problems are like other people's. Whether I solve
them or not is up to me.

> *Memory is the power to gather roses in winter.*
>
> —*Anonymous*

What a marvelous capacity we each have to capture and savor the bliss of past moments. They serve to comfort us while we're enduring the pain of the present. However, it's this present experience that has called us to attention. Within its context we'll be challenged to tackle the lessons for which past memories have prepared us.

Notwithstanding the comfort of the past, we'd do well not to hang on to past memories unrelentingly. Only by flowing with the present and absorbing how these events punctuate our lives, are we grasping the full experience our lives offer. There are too many people who live half-lives, and thus find half-joys because they fail to give up the past for the fuller measure that is offered in the present.

Fortunately, we are blessed with the power to live here and now, or in the past, if we so choose. Freedom of choice is the special gift of the human condition.

I'll appreciate my gift of choice today and linger in the past only as it benefits the better part of the present.

Everything's got a moral, if you can only find it.

—Lewis Carroll

To say that life is full of meaning is not to say that meaning is fixed or magical. Signs come to us from within, not from outside; the morals we can draw from the little dramas in our lives have to do with our own growth.

We can learn from negative experiences as well as positive ones, and we need to applaud our own progress (it's likely no one else will). Only we can know how far we have travelled when we overcome a fear of speaking in public, or joining a volunteer telephone campaign. Or perhaps we've learned to say "no" to the constant demands others make of us; we're the only ones who recognize that advance, and we deserve to congratulate ourselves for it.

Finding the morals in daily events can be an adventure. It's good to take stock periodically; it helps us to see what progress we've made and to scale our expectations to the real pace of our growth.

Today I'll hold a private viewing of some of my recent successes; I'll be my own best audience.

May 20

> *Our deeds still travel with us from afar,*
> *And what we have been makes us what we are.*
> —*George Eliot*

Changing cities, countries, jobs, or partners can't change what we are; that change only comes from within us, from deep searching and redirection of our values and behaviors. Yet many of us blithely hope that a physical move will work a spiritual change. Still others trust in the delusion that a new relationship can transform the self that has developed slowly over our whole lives.

If we like ourselves pretty well, we can acknowledge our past. We'll own the choices we made at this or that juncture, and we can see the results. But if we're dissatisfied with how we're doing, if we feel the need to change our lives, we must recognize that hard work will be involved, hard choices and some pain.

Feeling the need is usually painful in itself. Often it means we're ready for those hard choices, and much of the work is already going on, deep within. Only a little more spiritual housecleaning, absolute honesty about our motives, and we may accomplish what we seek to change.

Wherever I am, in the twisting road of my life, is where I'm meant to be.

*Obstinacy in a bad cause is but constancy
in a good.*

—*Sir Thomas Browne*

Faults, when they're closely examined, often
turn out to be the other end of virtues. Carelessness in one situation might be generosity
in another; secretiveness might turn out to be
an extension of tact. In most of us, positive
and negative attributes are related to one another like positive and negative photographic
prints. The way we see the image depends on
the situation and the light.

Quickness to anger can also mean quickness
to forgive, to understand, or to move quickly
in emergencies. A slow reaction time may go
along with thoughtful caution. Understanding
of ourselves will grow when we come to see
ourselves along a continuum, where the traits
that hold us back in one situation may be ad-
vantages in another. As we understand ourselves, we learn to love ourselves better, as
we deserve.

*Today I will look at my behavior to see whether a fault
I don't like about myself might not be the other end of
an asset.*

May 22

> *The ego is a self-justifying historian which seeks only that information that agrees with it, rewrites history when it needs to, and does not even see the evidence that threatens it.*
>
> —Anthony G. Greenwald

One of the larger struggles facing us is relinquishing the need to be right always. Only when we've given up the struggle do we understand that the battle is finally won. We come to see nonresistance as the quintessence of the power play. However, our need to be right is the point of real concern, and in order to let go of this need, clarity regarding the human condition is in order.

Few of us are sure of our worth, our necessity to the better functioning of the human universe. We falter and fear our mistakes, certain that they will enlighten our fellow travelers about our inadequacies. And so we bully others, covertly or with great poise, into accepting our viewpoints. We believe that ideas shared by others are more valuable, and thus our own value is assured. No one is served by these exercises in truth.

Might the time finally come when I will understand that my individual existence is all the proof I need that I am right—without the struggle? I can practice this belief today.

*"Living in the forest" would mean sinking
into one's innermost nature and finding
out what it feels like.*
— Marie-Louise von Frantz

Our innermost nature—that fearsome place
where our dreams dwell—what would we find
there? Crude passions, lust, rage, and selfishness, or a void, a sadness without end? Many
people do fear themselves, and their personalities are built on a shaky foundation of mistrust.

These are people who don't seem to confront
their feelings very successfully. They may have
trouble acknowledging resentments or desires,
out of some sense that they ought to be above
such human impulses. Unfortunately, it is
often the very people who have such unrealistic
expectations of themselves who surprise everyone with sudden violence. "They were such
nice quiet people," everyone says, after the
scandalous divorce or the suicide.

Getting to know our inner geography, our
own pattern of needs and fears, is never dangerous. The danger lies in refusing to know.
We can't build solid self-confidence on ignorance and mistrust of ourselves; only by loving
ourselves and acknowledging our kinship with
needy, fearful humanity can we grow as individuals.

My roots in the forest will keep my head out of the clouds.

May 24

Toleration is the greatest gift of the mind.
—*Helen Keller*

With immeasurable ease we are able to pass through difficult times if we are tolerant of the people and circumstances that are beyond our control. Toleration is an acquired trait, but one that's cherished once it's securely developed.

Toleration comes more easily when the real nature of our existence is understood. Our lives are purposeful; however, no two lives share exactly the same goals or path. Each of us is fulfilling a destiny that's designed only for ourselves; others' activities or manners will be fitting only to them. Peace of mind is our due, but it will elude us if we're ever trapped by our desire to direct another's steps.

Freedom to live the day fully accompanies a tolerant attitude. Precious moments that could enhance personal development need never be wasted on fantasies of controlling others—fantasies that can never become realities.

My achievements today can be many if I'm not wasting precious moments anguishing over persons I can't control.

*. . . my grief was too deeply rooted to be cured
with words.*

—Orinda

We give enormous power to words in our
culture. Most of us have given words the power
to hurt us, at times, and we have also given
them the power to heal. Many of us say prayers
that have a special meaning, invoking deep
comfort and putting us in touch with our spiritual essence.

Life deals wounds that can't be healed even
by these precious soothing words. For many
of us, there will be times when all our strength
is needed simply to endure, to live from one
moment to the next. At such times, silence has
more power than words. We're fortunate if
we've developed our capacity to meditate, to
empty ourselves, and seek the still point.

The wounded spirit shrinks from words.
They can never say all we mean, and words
always carry the world with them. We must
cultivate the serenity that lies beyond words.
It has a nourishing power.

*Today I shall remember that silence can heal the wounded
spirit.*

May 26

> . . . *the absence of love in our lives is what*
> *makes them seem raw and unfinished.*
> —*Ingrid Bengis*

Love expressed softens the harsh cutting edge of any experience. Whether we're the recipients of love or the givers, we still share in the promised rewards, the greatest of which is the knowledge that we belong, that others know us. We know we're not alone when we feel another's love, and when we have someone to give love to.

Independence and self-reliance are worthy attributes, and may prepare any one of us for survival in hard times. However, if they interfere with our awareness of and praise for the interdependent nature of the world, we'll discover that our personal survival is at stake. Our emotional, intellectual, and physical development is enhanced by our involvement with others.

The alienation any of us feels at this moment can be quickly dispelled if we'd but offer the hand of love and willingly receive it in turn. Our lives are rich and fulfilling in proportion to the love exchanged among us.

I will let someone else know I love them today and cherish the good feeling it gives me.

It is impossible that anything should be produced, if there were nothing existing before.

—Aristotle

Everything comes from something. All the organic compounds in our world come from four elements: carbon, hydrogen, oxygen, and nitrogen. From these simple ingredients have developed the marvelous chains of self-replicating proteins that fill the planet with jungles, gardens, farms, the swarming life of the sea, and four billion people.

Each of us contains all human possibilities within ourselves. Nothing that we do comes from nowhere; we all have the capacity for great goodness as well as great selfishness and blindness. The choice, at every moment, is ours. What will we use, out of our formidable repertoire of responses?

Most of us have a pattern of response that we are comfortable with. Our habitual behavior saves us from the discomfort of always having to make a choice. But in exchange for comfort, we give up a little bit of our spontaneity. Every once in a while, it's good for us to become aware of what our habits are, and what determines our usual behavior.

Today I'll take myself off automatic pilot and navigate the whole course in person.

May 28

> *Happiness is a byproduct of an effort to make someone else happy.*
> —Gretta Brooker Palmer

Self-centeredness aggravates the natural flow of circumstances surrounding us; too much attention on ourselves distorts whatever might be troubling us. However, focusing on others' needs diminishes what we'd perceived as our own pressing need. This is a simple principle we might all consider adopting.

None of us is free of problems. That's one of life's givens. Through their resolution we grow and ready ourselves for the next group of challenges. Each group survived enables us to offer better assistance to someone else who will confront a similar problem. Perhaps we'd do well to see all our problems as preparation for guiding someone who will come into our life.

Helping someone else is certain to lift spirits and foster happiness, but the unexpected reward is that the helper reaps even greater benefits than the one helped.

My happiness is guaranteed if I help someone else find it today.

*People noticed and respected families that
included many old people, knowing that in
those families must be industrious, wise,
and spiritual women who gathered good
foods, prepared meats properly, and made
daily offerings and prayers to the spirits.*
— Mary Louise Defender

Until the recent past, the health of her extended family was a woman's responsibility.
Perhaps the American Indians were unusually
wise in appreciating the health-giving qualities
of both good nutrition and spiritual practice.
We sometimes forget how important a tranquil
spirit is to our overall health.

Health, as a positive quality, expresses how
well we integrate with the world. It's measured
by the success of our detachment from those
things we can do nothing about, as well as by
our engagement with those things we can. A
healthy organism cooperates with natural processes and throws off insults.

More and more, we are taking responsibility
for our own health. If we live to a ripe old age,
it won't necessarily be because of our daughters-
in-law or our nieces, but because we've learned
to respect the balance of the body and spirit.
"Daily offerings and prayer," that is, daily meditation and spiritual cleansing, is something we
can all incorporate into our lives. Whatever
our life span, it will be richer and happier if we
nourish our spirit along with our bodies.

*Many sources of wisdom are available to me, and the
strong voice of the spirit sounds in them all.*

May 30

> *To live in dialogue with another is to live twice. Joys are doubled by exchange and burdens are cut in half.*
>
> —Wishart

We live in one another's company for a reason. The talents any one of us is gifted with are most pleasurable when used to benefit many. And each of us is talented in ways unique and yet burdensome if not shared.

Our personal growth and development is dependent in part on the contributions made by those we're in company with. We live better because of others' presence and talented contributions to situations affecting us all. Likewise, others are equally benefitted by our positive involvement in their lives.

We need one another to diffuse the pain and sorrow in our lives. Sharing lessens the weight on a single pair of shoulders. Sharing also reminds us that none of us is burdened in ways unfamiliar to others. Laughing together also multiplies our appreciation of someone else's involvement in our lives. Every aspect of life promises more meaning when shared openly with another. We could even say that no event is really integrated into a life if experienced in isolation.

I'll find meaning today in the company of others.

May 31

"Yes," I answered you last night,
"No," this morning, sir, I say.
Colours seen by candle light
Will not look the same by day.
                    —*Elizabeth Barrett Browning*

Circumstances alter cases. We all know that important decisions require time and preparation, yet many of us make them impulsively or on inadequate information.

When was the last time we made a mistake in judgment and admitted it? Whether it has to do with the color of our walls or the terms of a contract or the person we said we'd marry, admitting that we've changed our minds is far more honorable than going through with a wrong decision.

There used to be a saying, "It's a woman's prerogative to change her mind." It's everyone's prerogative, because nobody's perfect. We are all influenced "by candle light." To be too proud or inflexible to alter a decision, even when we've changed our minds, is a good way to set ourselves up for misery.

Joining the human race is much preferable to fighting it. I will be human enough today to admit my mistakes, and free enough to change my mind.

June

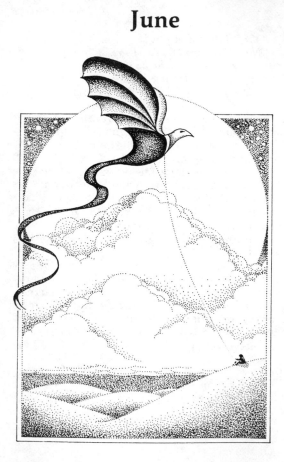

*The tail of the kite, it is true, seems to negate
the kite's function: it weights down something made to rise . . .*
—*Cleanth Brooks*

Without its tail, the kite would fly off in the
lightest breeze. The tail serves as a rudder, to
steady the kite and allow it to be directed. Every
force needs a counter-force to channel it effec-
tively.

Ancient philosophers looked on the body as
ballast for the mind. Without our physical anchor, they thought, our desires, our imagina-
tions, our ideas would run away with us and
the world would go to wrack and ruin.

Our minds and our bodies aren't two different
things. They're made of the same stuff. They
make up one being. We can never say where
one leaves off and the other begins, nor can
we say that one weighs down the other.

We can say, though, that we contain within
ourselves all sorts of contradictions, checks,
and counter-forces. This makes life interesting.
Looked at positively, it means that we can understand any human possibility because we
contain them all.

*Contradictions only bother me before I can see them as
parts of a larger whole.*

June 2

> *Our grand business is not to see what lies
> dimly at a distance, but to do what lies clearly
> at hand.*
> —Thomas Carlyle

First things first. How much more simply
life could evolve if we'd but focus our attention
on the obvious situation confronting us, looking
always for our direction from within the situation's elements.

How little point there is in worrying about
what may come, and yet we expend incalculable
amounts of energy in just such activity. What
lies before us is all there really is in our lives—
today. Nothing confronts us without purpose.
Whatever the situation, it has called us forth
to act. Our action will benefit us if we choose
to transcend the ego that invites our worry,
our smallness in thought and behavior.

*Today stands before me, awaiting my involvement. I
will go peacefully, addressing only those situations that
invite my attention, and I will give it, fully.*

Maybe if I listen closely to the rocks
Next time, I'll hear something, if not
A word, perhaps the faint beginning
*   of a syllable.*
                              —Phoebe Hanson

Everything in the world has something to say to us: rocks, garbage, even our disappointments and failures. For everything belongs to the vast, pulsating pattern that is the earth. Nothing that exists does not belong; if we find this or that piece of the pattern troublesome, it's because we haven't perceived its contribution to the whole.

Sometimes, when we're feeling down on ourselves, nothing seems to fit. What we're really feeling is isolated and sorry for ourselves—"out of sorts," that is, unmatched. Why do we do this to ourselves—pretend we're different, pretend that no one can understand us? It's a childish game, really; we're surrounded by pattern pieces that we match like lock and key, even the rocks by the cabin door.

I will listen closely. Who knows? I might hear something I need to learn.

June 4

> *No person in the world ever attempted to wrong another without being injured in return—some way, somehow, sometime.*
> —*William George Jordan*

Whatever our actions today, they will repay us in kind. Our choices will be many, as will our opportunities. Kindness fosters kindness. Respect elicits respect. A positive attitude clears the way for smooth sailing.

We create the world we find by our every action. No thought escapes the ripple effect. Each response we make to another, or to a situation, sets in motion a new wave of activity that will find its way back to us, in time.

To each moment we owe attention, and we have total power regarding the form and the manner of our attention. We can be certain that whatever confronts us today has its roots in our own past action.

I can be certain that to invite positive opportunities in my tomorrows means meeting those of today with kindness of spirit.

Anyone can blame; it takes a specialist to praise.
　　　　　　　　　　　—*Konstantin Stanislavski*

True praise is a form of love. Mystics and saints have seen the whole living, breathing world as a hymn of praise to the Creator Spirit. This spiritual vision implies that praise is both a natural act and an art; simply being can be a form of praise, and so can the most intricate skill.

When we praise another insincerely, we are often concealing other utterances—perhaps jealousy or fear. When was the last time we spoke praise with all our heart?

Blame is easy because we all know what it is to fail. And if we feel blameworthy ourselves, we like to enlist company, to point out others' failings. Why should we be so grudging of praise? Praise doesn't diminish us; to the contrary, it augments our spirit. We might seek out occasions for praise, as a way of expanding our lives.

I will do what I can to become a specialist of praise.

June 6

> *Rudeness is a weak person's attempt at strength.*
>
> —*J. Matthew Casey*

How others treat us indicates the self-assurance attained by those persons. Confident, content, self-respecting people are ably respectful of others. We often doubt our ability, either physical or intellectual, because someone has heaped criticism upon us.

The converse is likewise true. How we treat others at any time clearly reveals our personal contentment. We are not powerless over our reactions, even to pressing situations or pushy personalities. We can decide to behave admirably, which, in turn, nurtures all personalities and soothes every situation.

The adage, "we teach others how to treat us," is a wise reminder when we contemplate our actions and reactions.

My behavior today is an open invitation to others for treatment in kind. I will find responses that are complementary to my own.

Life is no argument. The conditions of life might include error.
                    —*Friedrich Nietzsche*

We've all known people to whom it was terribly important that they always be right. Perhaps some of us *are* those people, at least part of the time. Life under these conditions is an unrelenting struggle against sloppy thinking, dirt, carelessness, and the general slipshod stupidity of the rest of the world.

When we think this way, it is well to wonder how it is that we are right, while everyone else is wrong. We may find that our behavior is based not on rational thinking but on fear—the fear that if we relinquish control even for a moment, we'll fall into chaos.

How sad to be held hostage by such fears! The chaos we imagine at these times is no more real than the order we struggle to impose. What we need is self-acceptance—the humble but joyous recognition that we are human, just like everyone else, and that human beings might include error in their lives.

Perfection is an ideal, not a real phenomenon. Only by accepting my imperfection can I become fully human.

June 8

Doubt indulged soon becomes doubt realized.
—Francis Ridley Havergal

Self-confidence is not a given in our lives. It must be developed, often painstakingly, one task, one account, one deadline at a time. And each day that we court indecision and doubt, we erode not only this development in process but the level of self-confidence that had already been attained.

There is very little in our lives that we have full control over. We can affect the outcome to a situation. The dynamics of a relationship reflect our input. But in most instances of our lives, we offer only a contribution. We do not have the power to totally control the outcome. However, in one area we do have full power. That area is attitude. And the attitude expressed on any occasion will profoundly affect the dynamics of the situation.

A confident posture in one instance makes easier the same posture in instances thereafter. Likewise, doubt breeds itself. The attitude we choose to express teaches others what to expect from us.

What posture will I assume today? The one I choose will directly affect all outcomes. I can move forward with assurance.

> *The solution to my life occurred to me one*
> *evening while I was ironing a shirt.*
> *—Alice Munro*

We all receive flashes of illumination, messages like shafts of lightning from one part of our brain to another. *This is the answer! This is the meaning of life!* Mathematicians tell stories of equations solved in a dream; we cling to the notion that an apple beaned Isaac Newton.

We all experience moments that seem like the brilliant knitting-together of our fortunes. At such a moment, we are happy. We wish this could last forever. But the moment, like the illuminating flash, fades in intensity and is gone. The next moment holds something new.

What we may not remember is that these revelations and these moments of joy are prepared for, day by day. The slow building up of ordinary acts and thoughts prepares us for the flash of blinding clarity. The solution to our lives isn't a meteor; it's a mosaic, made up of many ordinary acts and choices, plans and reflections. And Oh, how sweet the flashes, when they come!

Because I am the source of the questions, I really do know all the answers.

The worst sin towards our fellow creatures
is not to hate them, but to be indifferent to
them; that's the essence of inhumanity.
                    —*George Bernard Shaw*

The greatest gift we can give is rapt attention to one another's existence. Of one thing we can be certain: we each are in this world by design. Further, we are in one another's daily travels by invitation. We share a destiny, and our understanding and joy will be proportionate to our sincere attention to those we're obviously accompanying.

No opportunity for an exchange of words, simple gestures, quiet thoughts should be discounted or denied. Each moment of our lives offers us the necessary experiences for our full potential. We need one another's presence, contributions, even tribulations in order to move forward together as well as individually.

I go forth today alone and yet in good company. Everyone here in my life now is part of my destiny. Our trip is planned for today.

*The mind is a baby giant who, more provident
in the cradle than he knows, has hurled his
paths in life all round ahead of him, like
playthings . . .*

—*Robert Frost*

Sometimes we are bewildered by the options open to us. We feel we have no way of knowing which course would be best. But when we reflect calmly on our choices, we usually find very few that are realistic, that are in tune with our personalities and consonant with the rest of our lives.

It sometimes seems that a choice made, or an option dropped, when we are very young, can determine our whole lives. This is probably an illusion. Perhaps we believe that our fate was forever altered by missing a train ten years ago. Late at night, we might talk wistfully of what might have been, "If only I'd caught that train!"

Most likely, though, our lives would have turned out pretty much the same. What happens to us, and what we choose, seem to follow the same pattern—a pattern that is true for each one of us. We've marked out our paths, whether we're fully aware of them or not.

Sometimes I am indecisive because I desire to remain open to life's choices. Today I will act freely and strengthen that freedom by making responsible decisions.

June 12

Two may talk together under the same roof
for many years, yet never really meet.
— Mary Catherwood

Conversation does not assure, nor even imply, self-revelation. Trading words is easily, frequently, and safely done; however, it doesn't introduce us to the one-another that resides within. Knowing one another can only be fostered by soul-baring.

Each of us needs to be wholly known by another. Only then, in the act of total self-disclosure, do we honestly confront ourselves. We learn in the process that our fears and our shame about our secret selves are far greater than is warranted. Silence about the "me" within distracts our perspective. Meeting another person fully reveals to both a new reality about life.

We cheat ourselves of the real pleasure in living when we hold ourselves back from someone close. Tearing down the barriers that separate us is exhilarating. Only when those barriers are down do we experience the full measure of the moment.

I will have a chance today to be whole and open with someone close. I'm guaranteed a reward when I take this opportunity.

Memories, like olives, are an acquired taste.
—Max Beerbohm

We've all learned to like different things as we've grown; different flavors, different colors, different music. There's no such thing as just naturally liking hockey or jazz; even if we're barely aware of doing so, we had to discipline ourselves to find the pattern of rewards in the game or the music.

It's no accident that the greater the effort we expend on acquiring a new taste, usually the greater the pleasure it gives us. Bridge is more fun than gin rummy; Bach wears better than Mantovani. It's true for other behaviors as well; the more of ourselves we invest, the greater the rewards.

This is nowhere so true as in relationships—the more we put in, the more we receive. A truly high quality of personal relationships is something we all deserve and too few of us get. We may settle for less than we deserve out of doubt or pity or the sneaking feeling that perhaps we don't deserve the best, after all.

The first and most important element is us—our own investment, the honesty and openness we bring to others, and the trust we are willing to bestow. Quality attracts quality; if we have trouble with our relationships, we'd do well to re-evaluate the tastes we've acquired.

I'll look at my part; the only person I'm responsible for is me.

June 14

> *There's a period of life when we swallow a knowledge of ourselves and it becomes either good or sour inside.*
>
> —Pearl Bailey

None of us is all good or all bad. Each of us takes pride in some of our actions and suffers shame for others. To be human guarantees upheavals; we are assured of shortcomings, and we can count on glad tidings too. Taking all of life's ebb and flow, smoothed by our own personal responses, leads us to a mellow maturity.

Self-acceptance is mandatory if we are ever to experience the sweetness of serenity. This acceptance must be whole and unconditional, not selective. We are who we know how to be at the moment, nothing more. But we are in a continual state of becoming. Whatever we've said, thought, or done combines in untold ways to enrich our experiences and the lives of those we touch. Let's not be soured by the self of the past, of yesterday even. Humbly accepting that portion of the whole will sweeten the rest.

I can avoid personal shame today if I think and feel before acting or reacting.

At Oran, as elsewhere, for lack of time and thinking, people have to love one another without knowing much about it.
—*Albert Camus*

What is time for? How often we say, "I don't have the time for—" meaning our marriages, our friends, our children, our hobbies, our parents, ourselves. Just what is important, anyway?

Some people seem to do everything in the margins of their lives, without thinking or knowing much about it. They go to school, get married, have children, get divorced, experience losses, get jobs, all rather off-handedly. Their attention always seems to be somewhere else.

All of us are preoccupied sometimes. And sometimes, in the middle of our lives, the preoccupation clears. "I woke up this morning and took a long look at my life. What have I gotten myself into!" Suddenly, somehow, our full attention is turned on the matter at hand. Suddenly, we have time to think. What's revealed then is the pattern of our lives. Did we make choices at random, irresponsibly? Now that we can see, are there parts to do over?

I'll endeavor to write my life story in the center of the page, not in the margins.

June 16

Hold fast to dreams for if dreams die,
life is a broken-winged bird that cannot fly.
                                        —*Langston Hughes*

Our dreams are our invitations to perform the dance we've been gifted with. Dreams are full of purpose. They mean to inspire us, acting as markers along the paths to our destination. Had we no dreams, we'd quickly lose the will to live.

The twenty-four hours ahead will be filled with dreams as well as actions. The actions we take today are no doubt inspired by yesterday's or last week's dreams. Dreams help us to image that which our souls desire us to do. This imagery is powerful, helping us to be prepared for any situation that requests our involvement.

Through our dreams we feel the pull of the inner self—that center we each have which knows our needs, our talents, our proper course and destination. We need to nurture the tie to the inner self; we can be grateful for our dreams.

My lifeline to tomorrow is through today's dream. I will respect its call.

> *The desire to believe the best of people is a*
> *prerequisite for intercourse with strangers;*
> *suspicion is reserved for friends.*
> —Mary McCarthy

How often we find ourselves treating our acquaintances with exquisite courtesy, while our friends and loved ones get our yawns, our sulks, our tantrums. We may pride ourselves on treating everyone alike, but most of us lapse into rudeness with our intimates. "It doesn't matter," we say. "They know me."

If someone doesn't know us, we behave with generosity. Why? To convince the stranger that we are nicer than we really are? Which is the real person, the one who is courteous to strangers, or the one who is rude to friends?

Mistrust of ourselves is the basis of these false values. Most of us fear, at one time or another, that we won't be liked, loved, or respected for ourselves alone. So we try to appear different, usually better. Once we're assured of approval from another, we feel comfortable enough to drop the façade.

Sometimes, perhaps, we even punish the new friend a little for the strain of our good behavior. Wouldn't the best behavior be a comfortable respect?

My friends deserve my courtesy as well as my love. Today I will welcome them gratefully to my life.

June 18

The greatest danger, that of losing one's own self, may pass off quietly as if it were nothing; every other loss, that of an arm, a leg, five dollars, etc., is sure to be noticed.
— Sören Kierkegård

Loss of self can threaten us at every juncture in a relationship. Self-love and self-acceptance serve as valuable antidotes. None of us is without the need for love and attention from others, and the temptation to buy that love by denying our own needs or goals is great. Dependence on someone else's acknowledgment of our value can be addicting.

We can build self-love. We can create habits that will foster a strong self-image—one that doesn't rely on another's attention to insure its survival. Self-talk is one tool that promises a changed attitude. When self-talk is positive, we will discover a more secure person. Another tool is imaging. When we image ourselves whole, happy, and at peace in our relationships, we prepare ourselves for the eventuality of that state of mind.

Today offers time to practice becoming a stronger self. My words and my thoughts are my protectors.

I think I must let go. Must fear not, must be quiet so that my children can hear the Sound of Creation and dance the dance that is in them.

—*Russell Hoban*

Often we hold fast to our fear, and it prevents us from growing. Life's ordinary rhythm carries us through good times and bad, but sometimes we fear the bad times so much that we try to hold back life's forward motion. This also means that we won't leave ourselves open to the good. The only constant truth is that everything changes. If we can believe in that, it will help us to relax our grip.

Our fear is even stronger when we think we are responsible for others—our children, for example. We want to spare them pain, and so we forget to listen to the Sound of Creation. No one learns from someone else's mistake. If we respect others, we must recognize that they have a right to their own dance. Their own spirits will guide them.

It is often hard to watch another stumble or fall. "I could have spared that tumble!" I may think. But I am wrong. I will trust in others' respect for life.

June 20

Change of scene has no effect upon unconscious conflicts.

—Edmund Bergler, M.D.

There's no running away from the internal strife. Whatever haunts us must finally be confronted and resolved if we're ever to grow and thus contribute to our world its due. When we keep secrets locked away, the secrets begin to keep us locked away as well.

It is folly, and yet entirely human, to think a new location, a new job, a new lover will cure whatever troubles us. The truth is, however, that whatever trips us up is at the same time trying to edge us forward to new awareness, and thus the next level of growth. Our troubles are tools for a strengthened foundation. Without them, we'd soon crumble.

When we consider the conflicts we encounter as opportunities for further development, they excite us rather than provoke anxiety. Changing our perspective can make the same scene appear quite new.

As I look out upon "the scene" today, I can control my response to it. I can relish it and grow.

May the new week come to us
For health, life and all good;
May it bring us sustenance, good tidings,
Deliverance and consolations.
— *Women's Sabbath Prayer*

Our life constantly renews itself; we celebrate the new year, the new week, the new seasons. New babies, new jobs, new homes give us occasion for rejoicing; the reunions with old friends and family, the strengthening of old bonds, remind us of other cycles of renewal.

For some women, their menstrual cycle provides a silent rhythm of renewal. Some people chart their biorhythm, hoping to tap the ancient springs of life-cycle energy that power the universe. Recovery from an illness, completion of a long project, harvesting a garden, even making a new garment, remind us of our place in the long breathing rhythms of life.

When we are at the end of a cycle, we sometimes forget that renewal always comes. When our energy ebbs, when all the trees are bare, when any effort seems fruitless, we may believe that we have fallen out of the pattern. "I'll never smile again," we think; "the sun's gone out—nothing is worthwhile." Depression for some of us is part of the cycle, and like hibernation or the shedding of foliage, it permits us to gather our strength for the next creative leap.

When things look bleak, I will remember that change and renewal are a law of life.

June 22

. . . . . all humans are frightened of their
own solitude. Yet only in solitude can we
learn to know ourselves, learn to handle
our own eternity of aloneness.
—Han Suyin

Being quiet with ourselves lets the inner
person surface. Acknowledging the inner voice
invites the comfort it can offer. Acknowledging
also gifts us with certain guidance needed by
our uncertain steps. Our quiet times away from
others nurture the soul struggling to safeguard
our journey.

In solitude we find serenity securely nestled
in the recesses of our mind. We begin to understand that all is well. We begin to see that our
way is being lighted. Only in our quiet times
can we fully hear the voice assuring us to move
forward, not alone, but in concert with it.

In solitude we find our sanity when the world
around us seems insane.

*I will go within today in search of rest and peace. I will
discover myself.*

All weddings are similar, but every marriage is different. Death comes to everyone, but one mourns alone.

—John Berger

What wonderful creatures we human beings are—so alike, and yet so different! We can work together; we have built the Pyramids, the Great Wall, the great cathedrals of Europe, the temples of Peru. We can play music, make quilts, run hospitals, program computers. Yet we can also work alone. Each one of us has the power to think, to plan, to carry out projects that are distinctly ours.

We are both interdependent and independent —and both of these characteristics can give us both joy and pain. Sometimes we feel burdened and oppressed by other people. They *need* us, they weigh on us. We think that if only they would leave us alone, we could realize our true potential.

At other times we feel desperately, achingly alone. Unsupported, abandoned, at such times we may think that, if only we had someone on our side, if only someone cared, we would succeed. True freedom, however, like true security, lies within us. We cannot get them from others; we must find them in ourselves.

I will accept either good company or solitude as the condition necessary for self-fulfillment in today's endeavors.

June 24

The grand essentials to happiness in this life are something to do, something to love and something to hope for.
— Joseph Addison

Focusing our attention outside of ourselves on hobbies, on goals, on friends, steadily bathes us with inspiration and enthusiasm for moving forward. And this movement, in turn, rekindles our commitment to all our attention-drawing activities.

It is true that happiness lies within us; but our discovery of this is only made possible by our willing involvement in the lives and experiences surrounding us. Those who lead narrow, self-seeking, self-serving lives fail to discover happiness. It lies beyond their reach because they've failed to reach beyond themselves.

Each day is as full and as ripe with adventure and meaning as we choose to make it. Where we look, what we see, do, and plan for, are in our control.

I am personally responsible for the happiness I discover. I'll help my search today by getting truly interested in what others are doing.

The woman I am
is not what you see
I'm not just bones
and crockery
                    —Dorothy Livesay

As our bodies age, our spirit remains young. When we look at old people, too often we see only the "bones and crockery," the disturbing image of brittle frailty that lies ahead for us all. Seldom do we take the time to evoke the ageless spirit of an old person.

Yet those of us who are privileged to have close relationships with old men and women see beyond the mask of age. What we often find there is a distillation of experience, sometimes wisdom, always keen memory, and almost always a fresh and ruthless impatience with hypocrisy and lies.

Old people are wonderfully shameless; they have no time for false pride or prudery. In the process of living so many years, whatever pretensions they might have had seem to have dried up and blown away, like corn husks or last summer's leaves. This quality is as bracing as sea air.

The very old share it with the very young, who are too new in the world to be polite. The lessons that old people can teach us aren't written anywhere.

Today I will become both old and young by seeing beneath the surface.

June 26

The universe is transformation; our life is what our thoughts make it.
                                        —Marcus Aurelius Antoninus

It's awesome, the power we each wield in the life that unfolds before us. The inclination of our thoughts invites that which we encounter, which is that which we expect to find. What we can become or experience is limited only by our imagination. Our dreams shine like beacons in the dimness of our minds.

Just as our thoughts can nurture positive experiences and outcomes, negative episodes might be drawn to us, too. We can be sure, though, that we use this individual power to create the flavor of each day as it's met.

Our attitude is the byproduct of our thoughts. It is in our attitude that we discover strength or weakness, hope or anxiety, determination or frustration. Alone, we determine whether our attitude will be loving or jaundiced.

The breadth of personal power is awesome. Today will be what I choose to make it. No more and no less.

Science probes; it does not prove.
— *Gregory Bateson*

We crave security. Even the most restless and adventurous among us has a need for bedrock certainty about something. Religion fills this need for some; politics or ideas satisfy others. When this need is answered, we can achieve a measure of serenity.

Where does this need come from? Nothing in nature is fixed or constant. We know that our bodies, our surroundings, the air we breathe, are made up of chemical compounds that are always changing, renewing, building up and breaking down. Change is the only constant. And yet, if our inner reality mirrors this change, we may feel chaotic and unquiet.

All great philosophies and religions share the image of a still point, a final proof. The purpose of meditation is to quiet the mind, to find this still point. It is a human need to imagine something beyond changing reality that is the real certainty, the real assurance.

In a world of shifting, slipping reality, where it sometimes seems that our identity is just part of a data base that one computer error could erase, where city streets and national boundaries change their shape every year, we need all the inner stillness and serenity we can find. Belief in constant values can anchor us. Truth is truth, love is love, and we are what we are. These things are always true for us.

I will cultivate my inner serenity; I will attempt to find my constant truth.

June 28

Anyone who limits her vision to memories
of yesterday is already dead.
                                    —Lily Langtry

The breadth and attitude of our vision for today's potential or tomorrow's dream, will profoundly influence what we see at this moment. We have the personal power to chart our course, to set our goals and to take the necessary steps for their attainment. We also have the option to walk backwards, stuck in yesterday's lost hopes.

Imaging the person we strive to be, coupled with clear details of the path we feel pulled to travel, is powerful preparation for the actual trip to our destination. Conversely, our progress to "anywhere or nowhere" is a direct reflection of our short-sightedness.

The strength of our power to create that which can be is awesome, thrilling, and demanding.

I look to this day with hope and determination to say "Yes, I can leap forward."

God did not make us to be eaten up by anxiety, but to walk erect, free, unafraid in a world where there is work to do, truth to seek, love to give and win.
—*Joseph Fort Newton*

Today stands before us with promise. It invites us to fully participate in experiences. That we are alive, that we stand present facing this day, guarantees that we are qualified to handle every challenge that snags our attention. And we need have no fear. The world and all that's in it is spirit-full. We are safe and secure if we'd but believe it.

When we look toward the day with confidence, we tap the inner strength that is ever-present. The more frequently we turn to this strength, the less often we are haunted by pangs of anxiety. Our trust in that strength heightens our faith and our understanding that all is well —always and forever all is well.

Giving up fear offers a freedom that will exhilarate us. Faith, trust, confidence will ready us for any challenge, all experiences.

Nothing needs to make me fearful today. I am here. Therefore, God is here too.

June 30

> *My life, I will not let you go except you bless*
> *me, but then I will let you go.*
> > —*Isak Dinesen*

There is something noble in the spirits of those who battle death, who cling to life. We are all moved by their struggle, yet perhaps it is nobler still to let life go when the time comes.

This makes sense only if we think we can look back on a life lived to the fullest. We wouldn't want to die without knowing we had stretched our limits, inhabited them as largely as we could. Not in a worldly sense, perhaps; spiritual breadth can be as exciting as travel, sport, romance, or achievement. It's the limits of our brain and heart we want to test; for that, we could live in one room.

Not everyone is blessed with robust physical health, but we all have the capacity for spiritual health and adventure. Self-examination and meditation are the tools for self-knowledge and serenity. Unknown adventure awaits us when we seek to know ourselves.

My spiritual journey is the real one in my life. On that road, the true blessings are encountered.

July

July 1

A Feather . . . might accomplish it . . . or a
Trifle done in the right Spirit . . .
                              —Djuna Barnes

Sometimes it seems as though a decision truly
hangs in the balance, with such equal values
on both sides that the weight of a feather might
tip it either way. "I was that close to saying no
—or yes—" we say, holding thumb and fore-
finger a few microns apart.

But that's probably not an accurate version
of how we came to make our decision. *That
close* may not be close at all; we knew all along
what was appropriate. If we let ourselves be
still and listen to our private inner voice, we
usually know what's right for us to do.

If we find ourselves faced with a lot of decisions that seem only a feather's-weight apart,
maybe we're not acting according to our ideas
of what's right. It might be time to reappraise
our values. If we're believing one way and acting another, it might be time to change either
our behavior or our belief.

*Any obstacles to knowing the right course of action are
within me, and so is the right course.*

July 2

When once estrangement has arisen between those who truly love each other, everything seems to widen the breach.
—Mary Elizabeth Braddon

Intimacy is a bonding agent that softens our exteriors while it hushes the inner rumblings and creates a need for itself. None of us is spared that need. Having at least one other with whom we are intimate heals us, keeps us honest, and strengthens us for whatever lies ahead.

When intimacy is absent from our lives, it's terribly easy to lose ourselves—to lose clarity about our identity, to lose confidence and self-assurance. And these losses contribute both to a strong need for intimacy once again, and to a heightened sense of the risk involved in being open and intimate.

Any time we break the intimate bond, we impede our progress as growing, healthy persons. Mental and emotional health is directly proportionate to how close we allow another person to be to us.

My emotional health today is in my control. I'll let someone in.

That has not half the power to do me harm,
as I have to be hurt.
　　　　　　　—William Shakespeare

Each day is steaming with activities around which we choose attitudes and reactions. Any one circumstance might anger us today, even though yesterday it triggered laughter. No event, within itself, has the power to determine our feelings or our reactions. How fortunate that this is so. However, we often pretend exactly the reverse. "He makes me mad!" "You've really hurt my feelings." With ease we refuse to take responsibility for whatever mood we're in.

A sure sign of mental and emotional health is acknowledgment of our personal power—power over our feelings, our attitudes, our behavior in every instance. When we celebrate this power, we are energized; we anticipate, confidently, the situations moving toward us, secure in the knowledge that we can make them beneficial to our growth if we so choose.

How much easier it is to face each new day knowing that it has no power over us.

I go forth today ready to take control of my attitude and my behavior. My day will be just as good as I make it.

July 4

> *I also had nightmares. Somehow all the feelings I didn't feel when each thing had actually happened to me I did feel when I slept.*
>
> —*Andrea Dworkin*

Dreams are messages that we send ourselves about things in our lives that bind deep feelings. Often we find ourselves dreaming scenes from our daily life, ordinary situations that may make us anxious. Sometimes our dreams are images like newspapers, account books, or video screens to show us our fears.

When the events in our lives are dangerous and destructive, we may numb ourselves so that we won't feel the fear or pain they provoke. But our dreams know; our nightmares are an outlet for feelings that we've chosen not to feel.

Our dreams will guide us, if we honor them. We don't have to interpret every last detail of a dream to be able to understand it. The symbols in our dreams are coded, and only we can break the code. When a dream brings us strong feelings, we can usually—if we're honest with ourselves—determine what it's about. Then it's up to us what we do about our lives.

My dreams tell my personal story, and all the feelings in them are mine.

*There is after all no obligation to answer
every passing fool according to his folly.*
— *Elias Canetti*

Often we behave as though we were in other
people's power—as though we were bound to
act in certain ways because others expected it
from us without their even asking, or our ever
checking.

Perhaps we have a deep need to please the
authority figures in our lives because we fear
we're not worth much. Let's say, further, that
our boss stays late in the office every night. We
may feel compelled to stay as long as, or longer
than, the boss, out of some wish to prove our
loyalty and productivity.

Most of us realize that a challenge doesn't
mean we have to fight; an invitation doesn't
mean we have to accept. But sometimes, especially when it hits a sensitive or insecure area,
we find ourselves blindly reacting to someone
else's unreasonable actions. We feel sucked in,
manipulated, powerless.

We can depend on our own power when we
trust in our innate value as humans, and we
will make decisions that leave us comfortable
with ourselves.

*I will remember to guard myself against irrational com-
pliance.*

> *Of course, fortune has its part in human affairs, but conduct is really much more important.*
>
> —*Jeanne Detourbey*

Our behavior in small, mean situations is ultimately as grave in its impact on the whole of human relationships as a major action taken in response to a large-scale crisis. No action or expressed attitude is void of effect. Though it may go unobserved at the time, it will be felt and it will influence another's response at another time.

Our influence on others, on immediate situations, on the future, is profound. When we accept responsibility for all of our actions, as well as our attitudes, our choices will reflect a widened perspective. The power inherent in even the barely perceptible thought is awesome.

My conduct toward others, my unspoken thoughts and unexpressed attitudes will have their effect. My impact today can be positive.

What loneliness is more lonely than distrust?
—*George Eliot*

Becoming fully trustworthy individuals, living up to our own ideals, makes easier the decision to trust others. And when there is trust, intimacy is possible. With intimacy comes self-love, then other-love, and finally joy.

Isolation from others is a choice, one that breeds new levels of insecurity. Familiarity with isolation hinders our movement toward others, a movement that offers the risk of self-disclosure. And it's this risk that nurtures the friendships that comfort us.

Self-acceptance and self-disclosure are intertwined. Our rough edges are softened and easier to love after we've owned them, held them up for inspection, and patted them before tucking them away.

Today offers new hope to the hopeful. Being rid of the burden of distrust will lighten my day.

July 8

Love is when each person is more concerned for the other than for one's self.
—David Frost

Loving ourselves is a healthy and necessary attitude if we are to garner the strength and confidence to move into our world of experiences each day. Self-love, when it is honest and nurturing, fosters compassion toward the others who share our experiences. Preoccupation with self is not self-love.

How distorted our perceptions of life are when, with incessant rigidity, we force our personal selves to the center of every experience. When we focus only on how a situation relates to our own lives, too often we lose sight of the lesson we might have learned. To look instead with compassion upon the needs and frustrations of those sharing our experiences will usher in solutions and will invite an exchange of gratitude which makes all expressions of love easier.

When we look outward with love and acceptance toward our fellow travelers, we inwardly feel greater love, too.

Any expression of real love today—toward anyone—will multiply my possibilities for loving.

It was only after the advent of the white man that we met people who did not understand about the uniqueness of human beings.
—*Good Day*

Human beings have been known to act toward other people as though they were things, objects, instead of subjects like ourselves. Men sometimes act this way toward women; parents toward children; the young toward the old. This behavior has been most obvious and brutal toward the original inhabitants of some territory that others wish to colonize.

As the world runs out of secrets, and no place is left open to colonial assaults, we must guard against this tendency among ourselves. We can see it in military organizations and in industrial production, in bureaucracy and in mass movements. It's called disrespect for the individual, and it's always dangerous.

Each human being is precious and unique. It injures our spirit to forget that, even for a moment. And when we remember it, we're better able to act in concert with our self-respecting fellows.

In respecting ourselves fully, we show others how to treat us; and as we treat them respectfully we acknowledge and enhance their humanity. The quality of human interaction can be so wonderful; why should we deface it by forgetting others' uniqueness?

I'll look for the same respect from others, today, that I show them.

July 10

By education most have been misled
So they believe, because they so were bred.
The priest continues what the nurse began,
And thus the child imposes on the man.
                                    —*John Dryden*

In the early years it often seems to the growing human child that most of civilization consists of saying "No!" Parents and teachers sometimes act as if that were so. Everyone who has ever raised, taught, or cared for small children knows what a totally involving commitment it is, and knows, too, that it is impossible to do everything right. Parents struggle with their children over trivia; teachers may punish small infractions and ignore large ones. Humans raise humans; if it were possible to do it perfectly, surely we would all be angels by now.

Often we are fully grown before we're able to let go some of the rigid rules we learned. Often it may seem that our task as adults is to *un*learn what we learned as infants. The "housebreaking" that has made us considerate to one another and peaceable in adjusting our differences may also have squelched some of our capacity for feeling.

We can recover our feeling selves, without violating the rules of society, if we can remember not to be afraid. Feelings are only frightening when we repress them; when we let them out and let them sweep through, then they are gone.

My feelings may be strong, but they are not evil. How could they be? I am a child of the universe.

*Persons who habitually drink water become
as fine gourmets on the subject as wine drink-
ers on wine.*

—*Alexander Dumas*

How fortunate are those among us who have
the ability to turn things around—to transform
liabilities into assets. Life deals them lemons:
they make lemonade, lemon pie, candied lemon
peel. They seem to be able to assess the needs
of the moment accurately and turn them to
advantage.

We are all different. Success in life probably
has more to do with expressing our uniqueness
fully than with suppressing it and trying to resemble everybody else. Who is "everybody else,"
anyway?

We can't respond authentically to the moment
if we're concealing the truth. The truth for us
involves our own unique package of qualities,
our own experience and energy, our own way of
looking at things. Freedom, for us, depends on
the choices only we can make. The proper appreciation of water is a pleasure that demands
discipline. We're totally unable to experience
this pleasure if we are wishing for wine.

*Human beings share many characteristics. One of the
most important is difference. Today I will cherish these
differences as one of the bonds that joins me to others.*

July 12

> *. . . he yearned to package for each of the*
> *children, the grandchildren, for everyone,*
> *that joyous certainty, that sense of mattering,*
> *of moving and being moved, of being one and*
> *indivisible with the great of the past, with all*
> *that freed, ennobled.*
>
> —*Tillie Olsen*

In childhood we glimpse the dear connectedness of life. The delicious sense that life is a
grand adventure mustn't be put away with our
roller skates or high school diplomas; it remains
as true for us today as it was when we first
sniffed freedom and greatness in the air.

Life holds so much! Every morning we can
open a package of "that joyous certainty." Each
day, as we trace our paths, we're connected with
all that has gone before, and all that is presently
in the world, and we are preparing the future.
Yes, we matter; we matter enormously, each
one of us as much as any other; our unique and
precious consciousness matters above all things.

The part we play touches all of life. Sometimes
we choose to join our personal strength with
others'; sometimes we act alone. But
we are part of the whole, linked by our lives and
our choices to all the others on earth, as they
are linked to us.

Today I'll be true to my heritage of freedom and nobility.

> *It seems that there is a direct connection be-*
> *tween creative thought and involvement in life*
> *and the production of epinephrine by the*
> *adrenal gland. When the challenge stops,*
> *the supply is turned off; the will to live at-*
> *rophies.*
>
> —Norman Cousins

Living on the fringes of activity is a choice we can make. Always holding back, rather than becoming fully intimate with another in conversation is a choice we can make. Partial attention rather than wholehearted involvement with the task at hand, whether it be reading a report, chopping wood, or preparing a meal, is also such a choice. Each moment we choose half-involvement we are also choosing partial death. The soul is nourished only by the rapture of fully experiencing the myriad vibrations surrounding us.

Attuning ourselves to "all that is" elevates the mind, heightens gladness, nurtures the creative act. Each task we undertake today will benefit ourselves and others only to the degree of attention we give it.

The joys today offers are tucked inside the experiences that invite my attention. Living on life's fringes won't bring joy.

July 14

If we try too hard to force others to live in our world, because we think it is the real world, we are doomed to disappointment.
—*William Glasser, M.D.*

The desire to control other people, all situations and each outcome to benefit ourselves is a human compulsion, and one destined to foster frustration. Our need to control others is addicting, but our condition is not hopeless.

"Letting go" is a learned behavior. Like any habit, practice will make it a natural response. Freedom to fully respond to any experience can only be attained when we have sacrificed the outcome to whatever the bigger picture dictates.

To be enthusiastically, creatively alive means responding to the pulse of the moment, which means following the unself-conscious inner urging rather than the self-protecting and consciously manipulative ego. Our burdens are lightened each time we act free from the weight of the ego.

Letting go of others will lift my own spirit high today.

Our ordinary mind always tries to persuade us that we are nothing but acorns and that our greatest happiness will be to become bigger, fatter, shinier acorns; but that is of interest only to pigs. Our faith gives us knowledge of something much better: that we can become oak trees.   —E.F. Schumacher

Most of us struggle at times with a sense of worthlessness. Sometimes this sense of being good for nothing leads us to self-destructive behavior; sometimes it is accompanied by self-pity. At such times, other people's lives appear infinitely attractive, and we may fancy that there are easy solutions to our problems. "If only I had two nice children, an adoring spouse, and a house in the suburbs!" we may think, or "Oh, to be single and on my own in the big city!"

The truth is, and we know it when we're not in a funk, that our solutions, like our problems, lie within us. We all tend to blame other people and circumstances for our own shortcomings. That's human. But we let go of blaming if we want to grow.

We have the power to transform every situation. If we feel trapped by a job that seems dull or a relationship that seems lifeless, we can re-define our sense of the trap. What do we want? What prevents our going after it? What opportunities have we overlooked, and what resources have we left untapped? If we're frightened by a prospect that seems dangerous, we can turn it into a challenge, and at the same time plan realistically how to protect ourselves.

I will remember that every seeming problem is an opportunity for growth.

July 16

Sharing a burdened heart with another who has the wisdom, strength, and knowledge to carry it, frees us from its weight long enough to focus on solutions.

—Liane Cordes

Our obsession with a problem, any incessant problem, keeps it a problem. Our focus on it destroys the balanced perspective that is necessary for a solution to become apparent. Sharing a problem's details with an interested friend clarifies the muddle. It also doubles the chances that a solution will emerge.

Holding onto problems, like keeping secrets, keeps us stuck. Our emotional health is proportionate to the freedom with which we willingly share ourselves with the people close to us. Sharing our joys doubles them. Sharing our burdens diminishes them. But more than that, it promises the discovery of their solutions.

Today I will share a problem, perhaps my own or someone else's. A solution will be apparent, nevertheless.

*You had better live your best and act your best
and think your best today; for today is the
sure preparation for tomorrow and all the
other tomorrows that follow.*
—*Harriet Martineau*

What's done is done. What's been said is said.
We can't undo the mistakes of yesterday. And
occasionally they create the barriers blocking
us today. However, we can make sure that our
behavior today doesn't contribute to unnec-
essary problems for tomorrow.

A negative attitude toward other people and
toward life's circumstances becomes habitual.
Fortunately, a positive attitude does as well.
The choice rests with each of us to respond in
ways fitting to the preferred attitude.

How much easier all situations are when we
are respectful, hopeful, and interested. Likewise, the trivial matter can become a major catastrophe when we struggle unnecessarily and
with carping egos. We make the world we find,
at home, at work, and at play.

*Today is mine to make. Let me choose my attitude with
care.*

July 18

Man is a pliant animal—a being who gets accustomed to anything.
—Fyodor Dostoievsky

The ease with which we adapt to our surroundings is, to some degree, a very positive trait. It means we are generally flexible. However, our pliancy may allow us to adjust to situations that harm us. We learn with too much ease to accept painful situations—maybe believing that time will ease us away from it, or that a bit of magic will transform the people and the situation, thus eliminating the pain.

Knowing when to adapt to circumstances and when to make a personal choice to move away takes mature assessment. It also takes attunement to our inner self—the "knower" of all right action. Development of this relationship with our inner selves takes practice, courage, patience, and the willingness to detach our minds from external stimuli for a time. Responsible choices are never accidental reactions, and they will sometimes usher in a radical action, at other times easy acceptance.

Today will offer opportunities to "go along with" a situation. I will be thoughtful rather than always pliant.

*. . . [I]f you listen carefully, you get to hear
everything you didn't want to hear in the
first place.*

—*Sholom Aleichem*

What are those things that we don't want to
hear? Mainly, we don't want to hear disagree-
ment from people who are important to us. We
don't want to hear that our children are making
choices we wouldn't make; we don't want to
hear that our partner believes we are anything
but perfect; we don't want to hear that our
friend, our parent, our teacher, our boss sees
anything in us to criticize.

Poor us! We know we aren't perfect, but we
can't tolerate hearing it from someone else.
Why should that be? We know other people
aren't perfect, either. Where did we get the
idea that we're supposed to be error-free?

To accept our own imperfection is to make a
giant step toward peace of mind. To accept that
the world is full of people who disagree with
us—some of whom even love us very much—is
to begin to achieve maturity. Perhaps we think,
or used to think, that we would be happy when
we rubbed out our last traces of imperfection.
That is not happiness; that is to become mar-
ble—hard, cold, and breakable.

*True spiritual progress begins with my acceptance of
my imperfections.*

July 20

*Our soul makes constant noise, but it has
a silent place we never hear.*
—Simone Weil

In an unjust, difficult world, our soul is often
in pain and weeping. Sometimes it makes a
joyful noise. But the silent place, the still center,
is one we may neglect. Like white light, this
silence of the soul contains everything, yet it
transfers the warring jumble of noise and color
into a peaceful blankness.

Call it acceptance or surrender. The stillness
of the spirit is the stillness of communion with
truth beyond change. It's silent because it
doesn't belong to the world of the senses. We
have spiritual knowledge that's ancient, if we
let ourselves listen to it, and it will nourish us,
if we permit.

For some of us, it's a great effort just to learn
to listen to the noise of our souls. We've spent
years blotting out pain or joy with alcohol, other
drugs, or rationalizations. We feel we've made
enormous progress when we learn to hear our
own soul's noise. But be assured, the soul's great
silence can be achieved. It's our choice.

*My spirit can grow infinitely. I trust where it will take
me.*

Grief can take care of itself, but to get the full value of joy you must have somebody to divide it with.

—*Mark Twain*

We share this planet that supports us. We share it with other living creatures, each one offering a necessary ingredient that nurtures and sustains the continuation of the whole. Every experience that involves one of us, involves others who also need what the experience may teach. We are not alone, ever. We are traveling a path in concert with others whose needs are similar to our own.

We can expect to discover joyous occasions and will undoubtedly be visited by grief in our travels. The latter will be eased by the knowledge that others, too, have known grief. Joy, on the other hand, is doubled in intensity when we acknowledge the occasion giving birth to it and then celebrate it with others. No day passes without giving us many occasions to shout for joy. Too often, feeling alone and lonely, we close our eyes to the wonders that could excite us. The most fruitful lesson we can learn is that we have fellow-travelers among whom joy abounds and multiplies when shared.

Today I'll look for the joy in my life.

July 22

As contagion
of sickness makes sickness,
contagion of trust can make trust.
                              —Marianne Moore

Attitudes give birth to themselves. Fresh ideas foster fresh responses to old and new situations. Each of us is favored with responses from others that generally match those we've shared, too. We should never be surprised by how others treat us. We have been their teachers in every instance. Giving love invites it. Expression of honesty encourages that, too. We must only expect that hatefulness and dishonesty will greet us if we've offered nothing more to others.

We should always be aware of the power of our attitudes and behavior toward others. They will bring favor or disfavor upon us. We should be mindful, too, that joy is contagious—as are respectful behavior, a trusting attitude, and gratitude. We are charged with the responsibility for creating a better world in which to live. Peace and happiness begin here, now, with each of us.

Peace, joy, and good fortune will accompany me on my trip today if I do my individual part to spread it.

Not the fruit of experience, but experience itself, is the end.

—Walter Pater

The end can never justify the means; the means is life, as we live it, in the present moment. When we read of aged paupers who die on a bare mattress stuffed with cash, we recognize their delusion; but at times we can lose that clarity and find ourselves justifying practices that we know are undesirable in the service of a desired end.

Means that involve injustice or deprivation are never justifiable. We cannot ignore experience. We may have our sights set on a law degree or a sports car, but the experience of law school and of budgeting for the car are what we live. The quality of our life isn't measured by our degrees or possessions but by our behavior. It we have love and fulfilling work, nothing else matters.

Let's concentrate on today; it's all we have. Within this day, we have many choices and a rich texture of experience. We can't control the outcome; the moment is within our grasp. We must seize it, savor it, learn from it; it is life itself.

If I were meant to live in the future, my eyes would have telescopic lenses.

July 24

> *Two great human institutions were apparently inaugurated together, proprietary marriage and the division of society into masters and servants.*
>
> —Emily James Putnam

Just as every generation must invent sex for itself, so every committed relationship must invent equality. The concept is an old one; histories and civics books are full of it; but most of us have precious little experience of it in our lives.

Unfortunately, most of life is some variation of a dominant-subordinate relation. However loving our parents and teachers, they definitely have the upper hand. We play games to win; we're ranked in school and at work. We learn to jockey for position, to manipulate, to get what we want from those we perceive as above us and below us on the scales.

For many of us, intimate relationships present a new challenge: how to get along as an equal. With no assumption of superiority or inferiority, sometimes we're at a loss. How does one act with an equal? Who gets to decide? What are the rules?

Emotional openness, honesty, and willingness to take risks can bring most of us to the point where we can share equally—or, at least, discuss the issues with a partner. It's hard to let go of our old place on the ladder—to decide to be neither a master nor a servant.

Rare is the experience of equality. I will let myself be open to it.

The question is laid out
For each of us to ask:
Whether to hold on
Or to drop the mask.
　　　　　—Martha Boesing

Do you ever feel you are wearing a mask? It's a strange, uncomfortable feeling. We mistrust our own face; we don't even know what it looks like, because we put on the mask so young. But sooner or later we must drop it and face our reflection.

Perhaps the mask is silent, and behind it we feel like screaming. Perhaps the mask is festive, and our own eyes weep.

The mask chafes and confines us, but it gives protection, too. We're naked without it; we have nowhere to hide. To summon the courage to drop the mask, we must believe in ourselves enough to trust our naked vulnerability.

We may take courage in knowing that everyone is vulnerable and afraid. By wearing our own faces proudly, we show that it's possible. Soon, masks will be dropping all around.

Today I will risk showing myself as I really am.

July 26

The principle of life is that life responds by corresponding; your life becomes the thing you have decided it shall be.
— *Raymond Charles Barker*

The attitude that we carry with us into a particular setting will greatly influence our perceptions of any event. Our attitude also influences, positively or negatively, personal interactions, and not just those involving ourselves. The effect of our message is this: our personal power is profound. We have explicit control over our own perceptions. We determine our own attitudes. Every moment of our lives we are deciding what we want to see, to think, to feel. And reflections will inform us that our expectations are firmly fulfilled.

How exhilarating to become aware of our freedom to think and to feel as we wish. However, with this freedom comes responsibility. We're barred from blaming others for our troubles. Each of us is charged with the responsibility for deciding our own fate. How we prepare ourselves for this experience or this day is individually chosen. Every minute we are in control of our perceptions, our attitudes, our responses.

Today is mine to mold. My attitude, my thoughts and responses will decide my fate today.

*Whoever is interested in life is particularly
interested in death.*
                                    —*Thomas Mann*

In this biological world we can see clearly
that death is a stage in the life cycle. In our
human case, we cling to the precious consciousness that seems to set us apart from the
rest of the natural world, and we see death
with different eyes—as an ending, often cruel,
and sometimes unendurable.

We do ourselves no service to make an enemy
of death; it is a presence within our life, and by
denying it, we deny a part of ourselves. Our
deepest knowledge includes a knowledge of
death. To experience loss and to grieve it are
the great common human experiences, and to
deny them is to make ourselves less human.

We live in a beautifully balanced system in
which death is a part of everything that lives.
The pain of our personal loss is ours; within the
greater whole, nothing is lost. Perhaps it is too
much to say that we will ever understand death;
the fruit of time and pain and healing is that we
will come to accept it.

*Let me open myself to the knowledge of wisdom, to which
death belongs in equal measure with life.*

July 28

If you find your inner conversation running along negative lines, you have the power to change the subject, to think along different lines.

—Martha Smock

Most of us carry on a continual inner dialogue. At times we're sizing up our co-workers or perhaps strangers entering the room. At other times we're being critical of our appearance, or a piece of work we've just completed, or of our capabilities to handle a new challenge that's in our path. If we were to log the minutes of self-talk and categorize them, many of us might discover that few moments of the inner dialogue are supportive or filled with praise. In fact, we often verbally abuse ourselves and others—a behavior we can ill afford.

Determination to change our inner thoughts is our first step, if we want to find greater peace and happiness in this life. We are under no one's power but our own, and we have chosen negative thinking for whatever pay-off it offered. Time will prove to us that the pay-offs from positive thinking are far greater. We tend to become the person our thoughts prepare us to be.

I will celebrate my personal power and use it to my advantage. Today!

. . . we have
grown into one as we slept and
now I can't jump
because I can't let go your hand.
　　　　　—Marina Tsvetayeva

Long, intimate relationships often confuse us. We may lose the sense of where our individual boundaries are. We confuse our desires and our pain with another person's—our spouse or lover, our parent, siblings, or child. When that relationship changes, when the other person dies or leaves or forms another intimate bond, we may feel wounded and desperate, unsure of who we are.

The blurring of boundaries is never healthy for us—although we may not feel the damage at first. Sound relationships are carefully made; we enter into them without giving away our own authentic responses to life. When relationships change, of course we may feel pain; but we need not feel the awful confusion that comes from having given pieces of ourselves away.

I'll adjust my focus so there are no blurred areas in my relationships. For me to love well, I need to know where I stand.

July 30

Everything has its own perfection, be it higher or lower in the scale of things; and the perfection of one is not the perfection of another.

—*John Henry Newman*

There is no "perfection" in the world, yet in another sense, everything is perfect. Everything has its part to play in the world's great unfolding.

Everything in our lives serves its purpose for us. Everyone we meet today will bear some message that we need to hear—just as we'll bring messages to others. We're all partners in this dance. Each move we make affects the whole pattern, and we respond to the changes made by one another.

Sometimes the message is a need for change. That message is perfect, too. At each moment we are where we need to be, and the path before us can be clear. If we don't see it, it's because we've chosen not to.

When we grasp the reality of choice and change, when we learn to live in the moment, we come to understand perfection not as a frozen, changeless state, but as a part of our perpetual becoming. May the next perfect moment carry us to ever more satisfying choices.

Today I'll strive to clear my path and to appreciate the perfection of each moment that I choose.

*We are whole beings. We know this some-
where in a part of ourselves that feels like
memory.*

—*Susan Griffin*

When we study biology, we learn that in every
cell of our bodies we carry our whole genetic
program, the complex set of chemical instruc-
tions for building us: our skeleton, skin, hair,
eyes, muscles, brain, genitals, guts. Every human being is born with a set of capacities and
responses that are as much a part of him or her
as the capacity to grow fingernails or to heal
cuts.

Yet deep in our language and culture is a habit
of speaking about ourselves as though our intelligence, our feelings, and our will could be
separated from the rest of us. We talk about "a
body/mind split," as though our bodies or our
minds did not fully belong to us. And all cul-
tures have the myth of a golden age when humans were fully integrated.

Much "civilized" behavior is bad for us—we
eat and breathe stuff that no self-respecting
animal would tolerate. Our lives can make us
ill: immobility, anxiety, and stress show up as
ulcers, hypertension, skin rashes, heart disease,
obesity. We need to learn to respect ourselves
as animals, and not to deny that we have bodies.
Our lives, like ourselves, are all of one piece,
whether or not we understand.

*My real golden age is now, because it is the only time
I have.*

August

*Keep your face to the sunshine and you can-
not see the shadow.*
                                    —*Helen Keller*

We make of our experiences what we choose.
We can focus on the traffic snarls while traveling to work, or we can smile because we have
a job to go to and a car to carry us there. We can
be angry because the washing machine broke
down, or grateful that we've been free, for a
while, of the laundromat hassle. Every experience offers us an opportunity to respond, and
our response is always a reflection of our emotions.

We choose to be angry, depressed, or afraid.
We can just as easily decide to be trusting,
happy, or confident. And the exciting realization for us is that we are free to choose whatever pleases us. Even though we've gotten mad
for years over traffic jams doesn't mean we
can't give up the anger. How liberating it is to
claim control of our emotions, our attitudes,
our reactions to the full panorama of our experiences.

*Today can trip me up or I can run with it, leading all
the way.*

August 2

Old folks—and here I'm talking about myself—need more than anything else to feel they are needed, that they have a purpose in life.

—Ruth Youngdahl Nelson

Believing that we count in the lives of others, that others need us and appreciate our contribution in the workplace, the community, and at home is a universal need. In those times when reassurance from others is lacking, we must simply remember that every one of us is unique, and created to contribute to our surroundings in individually inspired ways. At every moment we are leveling an impact on the physical, mental, and emotional environment of the community that surrounds us.

We are not without purpose. The daily activities which invite our attention are the paths to growth and fulfillment which are fitting for the contributions we are called on to offer. We are obliged to do our part.

My involvement in life has meaning. I may not wholly understand the part I'm playing but I can trust that I'm being invited, today, to participate in matters influencing a bigger picture.

Any idea seriously entertained tends to bring
about the realization of itself.
                    —*Joseph Chilton Pearce*

There is magic in believing in our capabilities
at the moment, believing in our future potential, believing that we are worthy human beings
with a purpose for being alive. Those ideas we
hold in our minds, be they positive self-ap-
praisals or negative personal assessments, will
influence our behavior and as a consequence
will invite others to form like-minded opinions.
We tell others what to think of us by our actions
and reactions, silences and outbursts.

However, the chance is present every moment to realize new dreams, to progress to new
heights, to switch whatever course we are
presently traveling on. All it takes is a changed
attitude, commitment to a new idea, and the
accompanying belief in the idea's potential.
Any idea held in our mind can become a reality.

I'll have a chance to practice believing in myself and my
potential today. It will open new doors.

August 4

Rivers and roads lead people on.
—Georgia O'Keeffe

Life is flowing and continuous; it is full of crossroads, tributaries, and sudden bends. To live is to travel, and navigable space attracts us. We want to follow the road or the river to find what lies around the next bend, over the next rise. The mere fact that they exist seems to tell us that we should follow them.

No one has ever lived our lives before us. This moment we are in a space and time that have never been traveled. Many past events prepared us for this moment, and we may often feel as though we were following a track that has been laid out for us; but at other times we feel as though we were strapped to the nose of a rocket, plunging through space where no one has ever been.

Then, at times (and we wish they were less rare), we become one with our path, immersed in our lives unquestioningly. This is the condition we prefer; when the river that leads us through life simply flows.

I will endeavor to accept my life; it is taking me where I need to go.

You cannot shake hands with a clenched fist.

—*Indira Ghandi*

Each person we welcome into our lives blesses us in ways that only the passage of time can validate. To invite someone in, however, takes an honest extension of the self, an open-armed posture which implies that we will risk being open.

How short and bland life seems when we cut ourselves off from the myriad experiences and acquaintances that present themselves to us. When we back away from the persons who have curiously crossed our paths, we back away from the lessons for which earlier experiences and persons have prepared us. Our progress and our success in life is both measured and nurtured by the number of genuine contacts we make with the men and women who are sharing our space in time.

Will I offer myself freely to today's experiences and personalities? The choice is mine.

August 6

So get a few laughs and do the best you can.
Don't have an ideal to work for. That's like
riding towards the mirage of a lake.
— *Will Rogers*

Human societies seem to go from crisis to crisis, fraught with injustice, oppression, and deception. But comedy is a gift of the human spirit. Sometimes it is the only weapon we have against official absurdity. Doesn't it often seem as though those who most clearly understand the dangers that face us are the ones who can play most wholeheartedly?

Laughter and play don't mean carelessness. Each of us must make our way through these serious times, carefully ordering our priorities and doing what we need to do to safeguard our spiritual growth. One temptation that besets many of us is to take ourselves so seriously that we begin to attach great weight to unimportant gestures. Humor is a wonderful tool for shaping us back down to size.

Sharing play is sometimes the only way we can touch another human being. Let us be grateful for the gift of true humor wherever we encounter it. It gives us strength to continue.

Today's events will remind me who I am. I will accept them with humor.

*There is guidance for each of us, and by
lowly listening, we shall hear the right word.*
— Ralph Waldo Emerson

Perhaps it was only yesterday or the day
before that we doubted our value to society,
or to our family or friends. We often lose our
direction. That's normal and consistent with
the human condition. However, the length of
time we spend floundering, uncertain of ourselves, is proportionate to the time it takes us
to acknowledge the guide within. We need not
be lost or full of doubt for long.

Going within ourselves may not be a spon-
taneous reaction for many of us, but we can
learn to respond in this way. And when we're
open to the inner urging and willing to follow
it, we'll discover the benefits. All that's asked
of us is the decision to listen.

*I can quiet my thoughts today, long enough to sense the
necessary direction to take. I can be certain the guidance
is right for me.*

August 8

*Everyone has a talent. What is rare is the
courage to follow the talent to the dark place
where it leads.*

—Erica Jong

Our lives are purposeful and the dreams that
mold our actions or tease us down new avenues
are not coincidental. Our dreams are messages
from the inner self, who urges us to fulfill the
purpose for which our talents have been given.
We each have talents to be employed in a fashion
uniquely our own; however, all too many of
us opt for the half-life, never fully giving our
attention to the occasion at hand.

We can never know our talents or when to
utilize them when we pass through life on the
fringe of activities. We cut off our awareness of
the inner urging when we don't enter into the
present, when we step back from ourselves,
when we refrain from offering rapt attention
to the "talent scouts" among us. And we'll never
experience the joy we deserve until we favor
the inhabitants of our world with our talent.

My dreams are my guides but I must follow them.

*. . . there are many sham diamonds in this
life which pass for real, and vice versa,
many real diamonds which go unvalued.*
            —*W. M. Thackeray*

It's high praise to say that someone is "genuine—the real thing." We use the image of jewelry when we talk about character: "Pure gold—14 karat—rings true—a diamond of the first water—a pearl." The qualities of beauty and rarity make gems precious to us, and by using the same language to describe people, we imply that real personal worth is equally beautiful, and equally rare.

Yet it's within everyone's grasp. We all agree on the valuable character traits: honesty, loyalty, openness, courage, humor, and the capacity for love. Everyone has them, and everyone can have them. Imitations won't do.

I needn't worry about whether someone else's qualities are genuine. I know what I admire and I have plenty to do polishing my own.

> *It is possible to be different and still be all right. There can be two—or more—answers to the same question, and all can be right.*
> —*Anne Wilson Schaef*

We're accustomed to thinking there are two sides to a subject: right/wrong, Democrat/Republican, walk/don't walk. This binary mode of thinking may lead us to disregard many possible solutions to our problems. "That's what makes ball games," we say, as though life were a competitive game. Relationships are an area where many of us fail to recognize that a question can have many right answers.

We may find ourselves locked into behavior patterns that guarantee we will be unhappy. We may set ourselves up as victims: "Everything happens to me!" or as bullies: "They all *obey* me, but no one *likes* me!"

If we look at our own part, we often can see that if we had behaved differently in a situation, the outcome might have been different. We often act as though we were programmed in a simple binary mode, yet we have the power to choose a new mode at any moment.

Today I will be true to my reality, which offers me an infinite range of choices.

When you are offended at any man's fault,
turn to yourself and study your own fail-
ings. Then you will forget your anger.
                                        —Epictetus

We take note of others' shortcomings and
frequently record them in our minds, and then
rely on these memories to feel superior. Seldom
do we perceive our own failings as clearly. It
takes courage and determination to inventory
all our traits, both the pleasant and the un-
pleasant. It also takes an honest desire to know
ourselves before we can fully assess the value
of our traits. We can be certain, however, that
the shortcomings we've noticed in others, we'll
discover in ourselves.

It might well be a worthwhile exercise in
personal development to let what bothers us in
others guide our own attempt at self-improvement. For instance, if another's cynicism triggers negative feelings in us, we can be fairly
certain we, too, respond cynically on occasion.
Then we can make the decision to clean our
own house. We aren't perfect, but we can strive
to like ourselves, and others. Self-improvement
and self-love will make it easier to accept someone else.

If I don't like something someone is doing today, I will
take an honest look at myself.

August 12

> . . . words are more powerful than perhaps
> anyone suspects, and once deeply engraved
> in a child's mind, they are not easily eradi-
> cated.
>
> —May Sarton

Some of our greatest adult sufferings are owed to the many innocent abuses inflicted upon us as children. Harsh words, demeaning punishments, too many silent treatments taught us who we were. Many of us remain disheartened, even diminished because of these powerful memories. When we accept criticism as accurate and deserved, it molds our characters, and eventually we live up to these assessments.

The good news is that we are in control of our own thoughts and attitudes, and in this respect we are all-powerful. The decision is ours to cast aside another's criticism, replacing it with positive self-talk. However, to successfully undo the harm others' words have caused takes daily dedication to our own positive reinforcement. Those who are confident and assured have internalized a positive dialogue with themselves.

Today is a new beginning, and I can make a fresh start by believing that I am a worthwhile person and my contribution is necessary.

. . . it is only by labour that thought can be made healthy, and only by thought that labour can be made happy, and the two cannot be separated with impunity.
—*John Ruskin*

We all require a balance of thought and labor, intellectual and muscular effort in our lives. The work that most of us do doesn't exercise either our brains or our bodies fully. Most of us aren't scientists or scholars, or farmers or dancers; we spend our working lives doing routine tasks and our leisure time on passive amusements.

It's within our power to enhance the quality of our health and happiness. If we look around, the world is full of challenges to our minds and bodies. We need only open ourselves to them. Other people will welcome what we can give—physical effort, mental gymnastics, or any combination of the two.

Ideas that aren't applied or tested tend to become anemic; and work that isn't examined and evaluated tends to become stale. We can't really separate our minds from our bodies without injuring them both. Our knowledge that we are whole, integral beings is precious; let it illuminate this day.

My spiritual well-being depends on living deeply with both my thought and my labor.

August 14

To find the good life you must become yourself.
— Dr. Bill Jackson

The more we run away from ourselves, the greater is our disenchantment with all the opportunities each day offers. When we live far from our own center, we insure distance from all the persons in our life. Happiness in all things eludes us when we become distant from self and others.

Finding ourselves, closing the gap on the distance created, is a byproduct of a personal inventory. We must *know* our wholeness before we can celebrate ourselves. And with celebration comes relief, freedom, and a readiness to tackle the opportunities presented to us.

Self-acceptance fosters self-love—the necessary prerequisite to the discovery of a good life. It's within reach. We must decide to move wholly toward it.

I can be excited about the chance to celebrate myself today. My qualities are special and deserve recognition.

*If politics may be broadly defined as "the way
we are with each other," then anything that
affects how we connect with each other is
political.*

—*Phyllis Jane Rose*

There's a word for someone who is democratic with strangers and despotic with intimates, and the word is hypocrite. One of the important lessons of our time is that the personal is political. Our behavior reveals our true beliefs and what we truly are.

"Politics" may sound like too heavy a word for our behavior with our families, lovers, friends, and co-workers. Yet it's accurate. If we oppress or manipulate those who are close to us, bribing and threatening instead of asking honestly and negotiating for what we want, then it doesn't matter what we say, or how we vote. Our weakness and lack of maturity reveal us to be unstable.

Our politics is our lives: how we connect with one another, how we use resources, even how we think about things. How we deal with the smallest details is how we really are, and others are apt to deal with us in kind. If we're abusive or insincere, we're going to encounter abuse and insincerity. Let's bring our behavior into agreement with our beliefs.

*Today I'll tune in to my political broadcast and make sure
it reflects my platform.*

August 16

*Any path is only a path, and there is no
affront, to oneself or to others, in dropping
it if that is what your heart tells you.*
                                                    —*Carlos Castaneda*

Our inner guide, our conscience, desires to
be heard every step of our way today. And the
choice to listen is easy if we've developed trust
in those messages from our heart. There is no
absolute path we need to follow in this life, but
some will be more advantageous to our destiny
than others. And some paths will weave themselves more smoothly among the paths of other
travelers. We are all moving toward the same
destination.

How thrilling it is to recognize that there is
a message center within that has foreknowledge
of our needs today, of the direction most fitting
to the growth that's in store presently. We are
not lonely, forgotten figures in this universe.
We have purpose. And we can fulfill our purpose
if we are acting in concert with our heart's message. When we move softly through the day,
we can be certain of hearing the words forming
within.

*I'll take slow, sure steps today and know I'm on the right
path.*

August 17

We only do well the things we like doing.
—Colette

When you were a child, did you feel you had to do everything you were told to do? If you didn't perform all tasks equally well, did you feel that something was wrong with you?

When we were young, many of us never were told that we were doing as well as we could. Or if we were told, we didn't know how to hear it. It has taken some of us years to learn that to do something well often means to do it as well as we can. And somewhere inside us, those children still groan over tasks they can't do easily.

It helps to remember that we are not alone. Something we find difficult to do may have all sorts of repercussions for us and for others. We can always ask for help. Other people are pleased when we ask them to share their skills. When we know how to console the child within, we need never feel inadequate.

I'm working toward the day when I can truthfully say "I like everything I do because I do everything as well as I can."

August 18

> *. . . the healthy, the strong individual, is the
> one who asks for help when he needs it whether
> he's got an abscess on his knee or in his soul.*
> —Rona Barrett

It is not meant that we should shoulder our problems alone. We are in the company of others by design, and the growth that each of us needs to experience is tied closely to both the sufferings and the celebrations that come to us all.

We each have the capacity to nurture and guide another's wavering steps. But the invitation to help must be extended. Perhaps we need reminding that each of us carries within us the remedy for another's ills. Likewise, someone among us awaits our call for help. We are accompanying one another on this journey because together we can smooth away the rough spots that would cause us to stumble if we were traveling alone.

Many calls for help will be made today, and some of us will be ready to respond. All of us need to remember that one of our greatest gifts is offering comfort to our stumbling friends.

Others need to help me—just as much as I may need their help.

A truly total history would cancel itself out—
its product would be nought.
                    —*Claude Lévi-Strauss*

The world has always been as rich and varied as it is at this moment. Wealth and poverty, joy and pain, peace and struggle have always existed side by side. The history of human life is the history of each person's journey from birth to death.

When we study history, we're always reading someone's interpretation or argument. The total history could never argue a point or prove an interpretation. We each can tell many true stories about ourselves by selecting facts from our personal histories. Yet our total history will cancel these stories and show us to be neither saints nor villains, merely seekers.

There's much we can learn from other's stories. They can illuminate our path; they can persuade us of the wisdom of one choice or another. Yet to be fully human is to escape the neat outlines of such a story. We immerse ourselves in life; we are surrounded by it.

I will try to respect everyone's reality, and to remember that much of the world lies outside my range of vision.

August 20

> *The liar leads an existence of unutterable loneliness.*
>
> —*Adrienne Rich*

All human interactions are built on agreement. Language itself depends on agreement: we agree, broadly, on the meaning of friend, blue, danger, cold. We agree on times of meeting, rules of procedure, and appropriate behaviors for many situations.

To lie is to break some of those agreements. "I returned your call" is a harmless lie, we might think, but if we didn't return the call, then we're lying about our intentions and our actions. It would be so much simpler for us to say, "I meant to return your call." So why don't we?

One important motive for telling such lies is to make ourselves look good. "I returned your call;" "I don't know how the paint got chipped;" "Someone stole my gloves;" all these are small falsehoods in which we claim that our performance was error-free—whatever slippage occurred wasn't our fault.

Human beings aren't error-free. We forget things, mislay our gloves, back into telegraph poles. We're human. Pretending we're not isolates us from the rest of humanity. Not only do we break the agreement at the base of language; we set ourselves apart from each other. We pretend we are more perfect than someone else; we condemn ourselves to loneliness.

Let us admit our imperfections; they are part of our humanity.

*Geese lower their heads when flying under a
bridge, no matter how high its arches may be.*
                                    —*Julius Caesar Scaliger*

Old fears oppress us. They can hamper our
growth; we learn nothing from them. Yet many
of us continue to be afraid, for reasons we have
long since forgotten, or never knew. Our bodies
sometimes carry the weight of these old fears; a
cringing of the shoulders or a knot in the gut
may be part of the legacy.

Our growth as free beings may depend on
shedding these old fears. They are as real as
viruses, and they make us ill in similar ways.
We need to examine our actions, to be sure that
we aren't just ducking our heads every time we
fly under a bridge. Am I behaving appropriately?
Am I meeting this situation in this moment, or
am I letting the past govern me? Am I acting
or reacting?

When we discard old fear, we have a sense of
liberation. Whatever wound that old fear was
protecting can heal. We are ready to face life as
it comes, not as we fear it might come.

*Healing myself empowers me to shed the fears that limit
my growth.*

August 22

> *Gentleness is not a quality exclusive to women.*
>
> —*Helen Reddy*

Our options for how we respond to the men and women in our lives are vast. Being critical is one option open to us. Indifference and gentleness are others. The way we treat others reveals our own state of being. When we feel at peace, we generally respond peacefully to others. Conversely, when we feel worthless and full of self-doubt, we're likely to be sarcastic toward others. However, we can pull ourselves out of the self-imposed dungeon of despair. The method is this: In spite of personal feelings, be warm, kind and gentle in every personal exchange with another, and your own dark mood is sure to be lifted.

Again we are confronted with the reality that we make our world. Our treatment of others treats ourselves simultaneously. Our friends and co-workers mirror the self we often think we're hiding away. A conscious decision will guarantee the happiness we long for when the decision is to be gentle, loving, and caring toward all the people in our lives.

Today I'll be as happy as I want to be.

Our greatest happiness does not depend on the condition of life in which chance has placed us, but is always the result of a good conscience, good health, occupation, and freedom in all just pursuits.

—Thomas Jefferson

Opportunities abound each day of our lives for respectful, thoughtful actions toward others. It's within our power to apply serious effort to any task securing our attention. Being concerned with our physical health and emotional well-being is also a choice. And we discover the level of happiness we attain in this life is in proportion to the considerate attention we give to others, to our personal needs, and to the activities occupying us.

The blessings we receive in this life are measurable by those we bestow upon the lives of those with whom we're traveling. There really are no surprises in store for us. We each must assume responsibility for our own happiness and good fortune; and there's no time like the present for opening our minds to this reality.

We sit at the controls today, and our perspective on the situations we experience will make them pleasant, productive, or problematic.

The choice is my own. I'll find happiness and good will if I foster it.

> *If love does not know how to give and take*
> *without restrictions, it is not love, but a*
> *transaction.*
>
> —*Emma Goldman*

Many people form primary relationships before they've had a chance to live alone, to be on their own, to test themselves out in the world. Sometimes, in fact, it's fear of testing themselves that drives them prematurely into a relationship. So a lot of early relationships dissolve. And if the people involved in them are motivated by fear, they're likely to form new relationships before they've given themselves a chance to heal or grow from the old ones.

In a healthy relationship, both partners give and take without restrictions. Love is a process, an unfolding intimacy between adults. It's no substitute for a mortgage or a Band-Aid. It's difficult to conduct this kind of relationship when we're young and unsure. We need an enormous amount of trust to be nurturing and vulnerable. After we've knocked around in the world a bit, we're more likely to have the strength to form a real love bond.

Today I'll remember to promise only what I can give freely.

> . . . *the greater part of our happiness or misery*
> *depends on our dispositions and not on our*
> *circumstances.*
> —*Martha Washington*

A light heart eases a hard struggle. A sense of humor takes the sting out of troubling circumstances. Likewise, a hateful attitude takes the luster out of the brightest moments. We have the power to control the flavor of the circumstances which will invite our involvement.

Accepting responsibility for our own happiness frees us from others' control. And it heightens our moments of pleasure. We are in control of the level of our joy and sorrow. In any situation we may choose to give others control over our feelings, but making that choice guarantees that we'll live half-lives with little real happiness.

Knowing that happiness is always within reach if I extend my hand for it strengthens my grasp. I'll practice taking charge of my own happiness today.

August 26

Life is terribly deficient in form. Its catas-
trophes happen in the wrong way and to the
wrong people.

—*Oscar Wilde*

Villains get punished and heroes triumph in well-made plays and books. In life it's not easy to say who's who; most of us are heroic sometimes and villainous other times. Our lives are an uneven mixture of triumph, reward, and hanging-in. Unjust events happen: children die, airplanes crash, rivers flood. The world contains starvation and abundance, violence and gentleness in its pattern.

The strands of right and wrong, good and bad, are mingled; there's no untangling them. What contributes to our personal progress is our ability to accept this bewildering complexity. To live wholeheartedly, yet to detach ourselves from the outcomes of our actions is the secret of serenity.

When a catastrophe strikes, we may be unable to turn it over, to find any good in it. We don't know all there is to know; we see only a part of the world's pattern. Hanging on to a disaster multiplies its effects. We must feel our feelings and let them go.

I will work for surrender and acceptance; the days to come
will hold brand new possibilities.

*Every time a man unburdens his heart to a
stranger he reaffirms the love that unites
humanity.*
                                    —*Germaine Greer*

Intimacy is the gift that bonds us to one
another. We understand our likenesses and can
acknowledge our differences in this process of
sharing ourselves. We can see how similar our
fears and our hurts are, and in seeing we gain
strength.

Becoming intimate with someone else unites
us, enlarges our capacities to nurture the people
in our lives. Our emotional growth is proportionate to our attempts at intimacy.

Too often we hold back from telling another
who we really are, fearing that they'll think less
of us if they know the person we hide within.
Only the experience of self-revelation can assure us that others won't think less of us. Our
unity with another is possible only if we share
the person who lives within.

*I must find unity with others if I am to have the strength
to withstand whatever befalls me. The people around me
can be trusted with knowledge of my inner self. I'll reach
out today.*

August 28

> . . . to have a crisis, and act upon it, is one
> thing. To dwell in perpetual crisis is another.
> —*Barbara Grizzuti Harrison*

Misery is an option available to us every day,
over any situation. We can linger, befriending
despair. It is also possible to take life's rough
currents in stride, responding to them sanely,
thoughtfully, trustingly. The rough times, we
can see in retrospect, teach us the most.

Crises become too familiar to some of us.
They push us into overdrive and an elation
accompanies them, an elation born from the
energy inherent in the crisis. However, this
same energy is inherent in calm, sensible responses to life, if we'd learn to cultivate it.
Crises ultimately burn us out, while measured,
balanced responses to turmoil rekindle belief
in ourselves, and our ability to handle the
gravest conditions.

Dwelling in crisis allows us to avoid forward
movement. However, if we want to grow and
find the real happiness we deserve, we must
move ahead to the challenges that promise us
our due.

*A crisis may protect me from unknown opportunities to-
day. It will also prevent growth. My choice is open.*

*We do not weary of eating and sleeping every
day, for hunger and sleepiness recur. Without
that we should weary of them. So, without the
hunger for spiritual things, we weary of them.*
—Blaise Pascal

A great spiritual hunger is a hallmark of our
age. Our age, however, is such a secular one that
many of us do not recognize this hunger for
what it is. We feel an emptiness and we try to
fill it with consumer goods or exercise work-
shops. Our restless narcissism takes up one fad
after another but, since we were not truly
hungry for them, we weary of them.

Spiritual nourishment comes only with self-
forgetfulness. This seems paradoxical; and yet
transcending ourselves is the greatest gift that
can be bestowed. Haven't we noticed that the
people who seem most at peace in the world are
those who live for others?

When we find a true source of spiritual
wealth, we can learn to satisfy our hunger. And
it will recur! Our needs for refreshment of the
spirit will be more focused, better defined, and
we will know how to satisfy them. We can never
nourish our spirits by concentrating on ourselves.

*I will strengthen my spirit by endeavoring to achieve
selflessness in my dealings with others.*

August 30

> *Don't do anything you can't share, and be*
> *prepared to discuss everything that you do.*
> *—Martin Shepard, M.D.*

Secrets diminish self-respect; they foster paranoia, and they make it impossible to have honest and open communication. Self-disclosure cleanses us; but an even greater benefit is that a commitment to it triggers careful forethought, and a needless or perhaps hurtful action can be avoided.

It takes only a moment to reflect on the possible ramifications of an intended action. And that moment's reflection can save us from apologies, shame, and embarrassment. Being committed and prepared to inform others of all that we are nurtures the growth of our better selves. No greater encouragement for self-improvement exists than the decision to share absolutely all.

I will think before acting today and find freedom from shame.

The reward of labour is life.
—*William Morris*

Almost everyone complains about work: the price of fertilizer, the drudgery of housework, the bureaucratic details, and the long hours. Whether we're mechanics or physicians or key-punch operators, most of us complain about the work we do.

Yet without work, where would we be? How would we derive a sense of ourselves as connected to the world, if we weren't involved in it through our work? Work is the fiber of our lives. It nourishes us and provides us with a measure of ourselves. When we're productive, we feel good. When work loses its meaning, we feel bad.

We owe it to ourselves to find work that fulfills us. We need the rhythm of tasks begun and completed for our spiritual health. When our work violates us, we suffer. Then we need to look for creative solutions to end our pain—changing the work we do, taking risks.

Work is our blessing. Today I'll be grateful for good work; what I do, I'll do well.

September

September 1

What is this life if, full of care,
We have no time to stand and stare?
            —William Henry Davies

Souls, like animals and plants, need air. Do our lives have enough empty space in them to nourish our spirit? Living in cities, plugged into networks of jobs, friends, and projects, we sometimes neglect our standing-and-staring needs.

They're quite specific: we need to be outside, in pleasant weather, with nothing much to do. We need to let the world go on its way without us for a while. We need to have things pass before our eyes: clouds, or boats, or waving grass.

Blessed idleness! Blessed inattention! When we slip back into the groove, we're refreshed by our passive interlude. Let's remember the recipe and find some time to stand aside and stare.

If I don't take the time, it will take me. I'd rather the choice was mine.

September 2

> *I believed what I was told and not what my*
> *own eyes saw.*
>
> —*Margaret Drabble*

Children see a flat world and are told it is round. We are trained very early to disbelieve the evidence of our senses. But there comes a point when we begin to question what we are told and to feel that our own vision is probably as keen as anyone's.

Independence of thought can be an admirable quality. It's also a quality that distinguishes those we call crackpots. Where do we draw the line?

It's important always to try to disentangle what we want to believe from the evidence of our senses. Wanting events to have a certain outcome can blur our view of what is actually happening. We can delude ourselves to the point of denying the reality we perceive in favor of some ideal, some fantasy.

Testing our beliefs against what our own eyes see and the opinions of those we respect will keep us balanced between skepticism and delusion. Life is rich and baffling enough without our fantasies to complicate it.

My uncorrected vision sometimes distorts my reality.

*The great thing in this world is not so much
where we are, but in what direction we are
moving.*
                                   —*Oliver Wendell Holmes*

We may feel idle, but we are not. We are moving along some pathway at every moment, and
each of us needs to accept responsibility for our
movement and determine our course. For
when we are not moving forward toward our
desired destination, we are moving away from
it. We are moving, always.

Having a goal inspires concrete action. It
fosters planned movement, a focus for the day.
Additionally, it facilitates decision making. Living without goals diminishes the joy that's inherent when we respond advantageously to an
inviting opportunity. Further, we can only truly
recognize essential opportunities when we are
in command of our direction.

It may be difficult to look forward to the days
ahead if we have no dream to shoot for. Perhaps
a goal for some of us is simply to choose a goal.

*I never stand still. I will take charge today of the movement
that's guaranteed. I will go where I want to go.*

September 4

It is only when there is nothing but praise that life loses its charm, and I begin to wonder what I should do about it.
—*Vijaya Lakshmi Pandit*

We lose our appreciation for joyful times when they become a matter of course. Compliments lose their delicious quality with overuse. Balance in all things offers the greatest satisfaction.

It's not likely that we realize the full value of variety in our lives. Probably we long for easy times, the absence of struggle, and certainty regarding outcomes. Were life to treat us in such manner, we'd soon lose our zest for the day ahead. The sense of accomplishment that we hunger for is nestled within the day's rough ripples.

Our experience in this life is purposeful, which means there are matters we'll be asked to attend to. Not every involvement will provide pleasure. Some, in fact, will inflict pain, but we'll discover elements that will enhance our self-awareness. Through this knowledge we'll find lasting fulfillment.

Today will be a mixture of joy, boredom, perhaps both pain and sorrow. Each element will give me reason for growth.

September 5

I accept life unconditionally. . . . Most people ask for happiness on condition. Happiness can only be felt if you don't set any condition.

—Arthur Rubenstein

When life offers you lemons, make lemonade, so the saying goes. It's simple and true. No matter the circumstances of our lives, we can maximize the positive events. More importantly, we can learn from the negative ones. In reflections on the past, we are frequently surprised to discover that the lemon made possible the deliciousness of a present experience.

All events of our lives are threads, weaving a pattern that is unfolding by design. Each experience is equal to every other experience. We shouldn't cling to any one of them, or shrink from any. It's their sum that makes us who we are. Each of us is a mosaic unto ourselves. And yet, by design, our patterns, our lives intersect.

An expectation that an experience is a necessary part of our design will foster gratitude, even in the moment that we must swallow the bitter fruit.

Today I'll be faced with some lemons. Can I make lemonade?

September 6

A depressing and difficult passage has prefaced every new page I have turned in life.
—Charlotte Brontë

What would it be like to shed our old skin, like a snake, when it grew too small? Perhaps the discomfort we feel at each new stage of growth is something like that feeling. Truly, each new page or stage of life has a difficult introduction—but if we can only remember that, it may help us through the bad times.

Too often, in the grip of change, we lose sight of what we are becoming. Did you ever wonder how it would feel to be a grub and then turn into a winged creature? It helps us to endure the depressing passage if we can remember that we're being prepared for a new stage of our lives, one in which, perhaps, we will leave our old selves as far behind as the dragonfly leaves the larva.

With time and wisdom comes the knowledge that some pain always accompanies growth. We can accept the pain more gracefully if we remind ourselves that we are preparing to turn a new page.

My spirit, like my body, holds the secrets of growth and change.

Tomorrow doesn't matter for I have lived today.

—Horace

The twenty-four hours lying ahead is all we have been promised. With that promise is a guarantee that we will greet opportunities for growth that have their roots in yesterday. Our evolution is not without purpose and design; therefore, we need not concern ourselves with the future. It will educate and comfort us as it becomes the present.

When we understand that the situations inviting our responses today have purpose, our anxiety is eased. Fear is allayed when our understanding is complete. Our life experiences are not happenstance, of this we can be sure; there exists an interdependence. Events are woven together for our greater good. Moreover, no one event offers more than a glance at the whole picture. So what we see today enlightens us about yesterday and last week, even last year, perhaps. Tomorrow will do likewise. But today is our only concern. It will provide exactly those opportunities we need to weave the next portion of our chosen design.

I am peaceful. Today will take care of my needs.

September 8

To dream what one dreams is neither wise nor foolish, successful nor unsuccessful. No precautions can be taken against it, except, perhaps, that of remaining permanently awake.

—Margaret MacDonald

Dreams, like desires and feelings, simply happen. They happen to everyone from early childhood to old age; they're part of the life of the human mind, and we can't really control them. All we ever can control is our behavior—how we act on our dreams, our desires, and our feelings.

At times some of us try to control the uncontrollable, and stay "permanently awake," to fence out or repress the sadness, desire, or rage that we don't want to feel. By doing this, we make ourselves doubly unhappy; for human beings are creatures of feeling and fumbling. To try to engineer the unruly parts out of our lives is just to create another way to feel bad, for the attempt is doomed to fail.

Accepting our roughness, the violence and vulnerability that live within us, is to let go of shame. Why be ashamed? All others are the same as we. We can't choose our feelings, but we can choose how—or whether—we express them.

If I fence out my dreams and feelings, I turn them into enemies.

> *When we cling to pain we end up punishing ourselves.*
> —*Leo F. Buscaglia*

Painful situations, relationships that hurt us, memories of experiences that pinch our nerve endings need not imprison us. However, we are seldom very quick to let go of the pain. Instead, we become obsessed with it, the precipitating circumstances, and the longed-for, but often missed outcome. We choose to wallow in the pain, rather than learn from it. And we salt our own wounds every time we indulge the desire to replay the circumstances that triggered the pain.

Pain can't be avoided. It's as natural as joy. In fact, we understand joy in contrast to the experiences of pain. Each offers breadth to our lives. And both strengthen us. Our maturity is proportionate to our acceptance of all experiences. In retrospect we can be grateful for pain, for it offered us many gifts in disguise.

I can see pain as part of a bigger picture, if I so desire.

September 10

I was tender and often, true;
Ever a prey to coincidence,
Always I knew the consequence;
Always saw what the end would be.
We're as Nature made us—hence
I loved them until they loved me.
                                    —Dorothy Parker

Did Nature really make us so that we despise those who love us? Groucho Marx's joke, "I wouldn't belong to any club that would have me for a member," implies the same thing. But this can't be; we're children of the universe, each of us exactly as lovable and fallible as all the others.

Many of us go through years of upheaval in which we want only what we can't get. If we should get it, heaven forbid, it turns to rubbish in our hands. Some people call this the "reverse Midas touch," and it's common enough so that we all recognize it.

This is a symptom of self-mistrust, of self-dislike. If we believe in ourselves, we'll evaluate those who are drawn to us on their merits. For someone to love us doesn't automatically mean that they're deluded. It might simply mean that they love us.

If I don't love and value myself, I won't really be able to love back someone who does.

We saw endurance, chance, and law. We knew transience but glimpsed eternity. We learned that nature's flux is constancy and we were at ease.
        —Edna Hong and Howard Hong

Precious are the glimpses we get into the nature of things. But we must be ready for them, or the most exquisite lessons will be lost on us. Anxiety, regret, or egotism can cloud our perceptions. We only learn when we can set aside our preoccupations.

To be hung-up is to be caught, like a coat on a hook, unfree. When we're hung up, our attention is somewhere else; we can't learn anything. And hangups are a choice we make. If we choose the freedom to experience nature's flux, we can slip off the hook.

Mainly we choose to stay hung up out of fear—fear of the unknown and perhaps fear of freedom. If we've spent most of our lives on one hook or another, we may not have much confidence that we can get along by ourselves. But we can.

Today I'll choose freedom and groundedness. I'll choose to learn ease.

September 12

The change of one simple behavior can affect other behaviors and thus change many things.
—Jean Baer

The effects on every action are far-reaching. Our response to a particular set of circumstances will influence its outcome and the lives of all persons concerned. Harsh words one time, a smile and praise another will make their mark in the system that includes us all. Our actions and interactions are interdependent, each one having been affected by preceding actions and in turn affecting those that follow.

A single action has impact on our subsequent actions. An angry retort is likely to influence our behavior toward the next unsuspecting person who gains our attention.

A grateful attitude expressed will soften the harsh realities of life for the giver as well as the receiver. The principle underlying all behavior is that it breeds itself repeatedly. Positive, respectful action can become habitual.

Let me remember that I'm creating habits by my every action today. I can make them good ones as easily as bad ones.

*To live is not merely to breathe, it is to act;
it is to make use of our organs, senses, fac-
ulties, of all those parts of ourselves which
give us the feeling of existence.*
                              —Jean-Jacques Rousseau

We are gifted with talents that need encouragement in order to blossom. Few of us fully
appreciate our talents. Many of us fail to utilize
them. And yet they are waiting for the invitation to present themselves.

We have been blessed with particular talents
because the world we live in needs our individual involvement. Each of us is charged with
a responsibility to contribute to the lives around
us. Our shared talents make the road smooth,
when each of us has acted as the need arose.

We are called to participate by our talents.
They help define who we are. They affirm that
we count, that we are needed. No one is without a capability, a characteristic that lends just
the right flavor to a situation involving others.
Whether it's a sense of humor, the ability to
write or paint, or a talent for settling disputes,
we each have a calling card, and we are asked,
daily, to make our contribution.

*Am I willing today to participate fully in the life around
me?*

September 14

Out of every crisis comes the chance to be reborn. . . .

—Nena O'Neill

It is not our smooth passages that reveal new understandings, but the strenuous, uphill battles that benefit us with the knowledge we need to grow. Looking on our challenges as gifts whose resolution promises greater comfort makes them agreeable, perhaps even prized. Without them we stagnate, and life's joys are few.

Life is a series of lessons. And our crises are our homework. The patience and the trust we developed while living through last week's crisis has prepared us for greater benefits from those that lie ahead. Knowing that a crisis guarantees us the growth we deserve makes its sting endurable.

Every crisis is followed by a time of easy stepping. These restful periods let us adjust to our new stage of development, and they invite us to store up our strength, our energy for the tests that lie ahead.

Every stage of an experience has its roots in the past and leans toward the future. I'll trust that whatever I encounter today I'm prepared for and will benefit from.

*It is astounding . . . how much energy the
body is capable of pouring out and then
replenishing. That is a magical act, because
you never really understand where all that
energy comes from.*

—Robert Bly

The energy and persistence of a motivated
person are truly marvelous. The work that
nourishes us, the work that is a form of rapture,
a form of praise, is magical. Where does our
energy come from? Surely not from breakfast
cereal, sandwiches, or coffee. It is a magical
transformation of earthly food into pure spirit.
Rapture isn't our daily state, but we can
achieve it. We achieve this rapt state when we
forget ourselves, when we're totally immersed
in the work that transforms us—whether it's
clearing a field, playing a cello, collecting stamps,
factoring an equation, or kneading dough.

If we're lucky, we discover this capacity for
transformation while we're young. Some of
us spend our whole lives searching for it. Most
of us come upon it somehow: the key to releasing our limitless energy of mind or body. Self-
forgetfulness is basic to it. The strength of the
spirit does the rest.

*When energy flags, it's often because I'm preoccupied
with self. To renew my energy, all I need do is get out of
my own way.*

September 16

*We are not educated: most of us cannot read
or write. But we are strong because we are
close to the earth and we know what matters.*
　　　　　　　　　　　　—Mie Amano

The important thing in life is to know what
matters for us. Our reality and values are our
own; no one else can dictate them to us. They
come out of our experiences and observation,
and our spiritual health asks that we be true
to them.

Similarly, we must be true to what matters
for us. We won't try to win anyone over. Nor
will we let someone else sway us. We will respect each other's reality, for that's how we
will live in peace.

Further, if we're open and frank with each
other, and with everyone else, we can spread
integrity, respect, and peace. Quakers have
a saying, "Let it begin with me." Integrity will
spread outward, in concentric rings, for we
are connected with one another.

Strength and growth come from knowing
ourselves, knowing what matters for us. If we
respect each other, we will find the way to fit
any apparent conflict into a broader system
that can accommodate us both.

If I am honest with myself, I can be my own best teacher.

*Things are in the saddle
And ride mankind.*
                    —*Ralph Waldo Emerson*

Some of us buy expensive toys on impulse; tire of them quickly; and let ourselves feel hopeless and inadequate because the impulsive wish was a shallow one. To ease our pain, we buy new toys—and so it goes.

Each new thing we acquire means new responsibilities: insurance policies, computer software, installment payments, safe deposit boxes. Deadlines and taxes oppress us; we dream of "getting away from it all."

At some point, we chose everything in our lives. If we wish, we can choose to do without it. When we feel suffocated by our possessions and obligations, it's good to clear our minds and think about what we really want. Many of us don't think about our values consciously until they become a source of pain.

We'd be kinder to ourselves if we were fully aware of our values when we make choices in our lives. Are we choosing things as a shortcut to happiness—or a substitute for it? If we feel an emptiness that we've tried to fill with things, we'd do better to tend our spirits.

Let me learn to trust myself; then I know I'll like what I do.

September 18

We are only as sick as the secrets we keep.
—Anonymous

Not letting others know who we really are keeps us continually off balance while in their presence. Risking full openness, even with friends, is not easy; however, the pain that accompanies secret-keeping far exceeds the potential pain of self-revelation.

There are unexpected gifts for our complete honesty. One is discovering that we're like others. We're not unique in our shame nor our self-abhorrence. And the attachments to others inspired by our decision to share ourselves strengthen us. The pain of alienation diminishes. We begin to sense our equality, one with another, and we experience trust.

Sharing secrets, our own and others', lessens the burden of guilt that diminishes each of us. But more than that, our freedom from secrets nurtures healthy personal growth. Hiding nothing convinces us that we have nothing to hide, thus we're free to try new behaviors, move in unfamiliar directions.

My burdens are only as heavy as the secrets I hang on to.

*It isn't for the moment you are stuck that
you need courage, but for the long uphill
climb back to sanity and faith and security.*
— *Anne Morrow Lindbergh*

It's not just major challenges that require
courage. Even the minor skirmishes with life
demand some deep breaths, perhaps hushed
prayers, and lots of hope. We'd glide more easily
through every day if we'd accept that struggle
is part of the process of life; that it offers more
opportunities for us to realize our individual
potential than any other dimension of life.

Struggles strengthen us, enrich our character, temper our emotions. They enhance our
being in untold ways, and yet we plead to be
spared them. How ironic that we each long for
greater success, at least some recognition for
our accomplishments, but recoil from the very
experiences that guarantee these personal
satisfactions.

*My struggles today are my gifts in disguise. I will grow
accordingly.*

September 20

*We succeed in enterprises which demand
the positive qualities we possess, but we
excel in those which can also make use of
our defects.*

—*Alexis de Tocqueville*

Those areas of our lives we struggle with
the most, such as impatience, control, energy,
or procrastination, offer us opportunities for
great victories. But even more, they offer
greater learning, and the greatest chance for
further growth and development when we relinquish our struggle. We can be certain that
any activity attracting our involvement will
provide chances to demonstrate both our positive qualities and our defects.

Our human need to be rid of defects can
hamper our progress, keeping us stuck in old
behavior. But when we've come to accept defects as normal we can even capitalize on them.
They define who we are momentarily. We need
to remember that defects are generally assets
that have become twisted with use. Therefore,
we can understand their origin and smooth off
the rough edges. Assets and defects will switch
places in our repertoire. We can use each for
the greater good of the enterprise deserving
our attention.

Defects have so much to teach us. They offer
us meaningful opportunities for growth and
mature action. Today's assets were yesterday's
defects and where we stumble today, tomorrow
we'll glide.

*My defects will offer me new learning today if I relinquish
my incessant urge to be free of them.*

September 21

To expect life to be tailored to our specifications is to invite frustration.
—*Anonymous*

Life is what it is. It seldom matches our hopes and dreams, but it never fails to be exactly what we need. We are shortsighted, really. Reflections on the past can enlighten us to this fact. Seldom does any plan develop as we'd assumed.

Perhaps we are only beginning to realize that there exists a carefully orchestrated plan that each of us has been invited to experience. Our contributions help to form the plan which enhances our personal development. We are privy to the tiniest segment at any one moment, however. We must trust that the plan has our best interests at heart, even though our sights may be focused elsewhere. The evolution of our lives, often in spite of our own misguided efforts, should convince us that we can let go of the reins.

What life offers today is what I need—no matter what I may think!

September 22

Speak your truth quietly and clearly; and listen to others, even to the dull and the ignorant; they too have their story.
— *Max Ehrmann*

We have been invited to share ourselves in this phenomenon called life. We are not fully cognizant of the value of our gifts to one another. We don't know which words we mutter might be the pearls of wisdom for another. However, we can be certain that we'll show the way to someone else. Each of us is acting as a guide for another, perhaps a friend, perhaps an enemy. Whenever the student is ready, a teacher will appear. We are all students. We are all teachers.

How reassuring to know that we have a story that counts in someone else's unfolding. And it's equally exciting to contemplate how another's progress will nurture our own. But we need another's attention in order to be certain that our movements are in the right direction.

I can't be certain whose story I need most to hear today. I can only be attentive to them all.

September 23

> . . . *we both want a joy of undeep and un-*
> *abiding things . . .*
> —*Gwendolyn Brooks*

When I can live fully in each moment, I can open myself to beauties that might otherwise escape me entirely. The more attuned I am to what is really going on right now, which means unhooking my mind from preoccupation with the past and worry about the future, the freer I am to catch fleeting perceptions and subtle shifts in the world about me.

We know that we only use about ten percent of our brain's capacity for the ordinary business of living, which includes building space shuttles and filing tax returns. The more fully we can bring all of ourselves to each moment, the more of our capacity is available for living.

Life isn't last year, or ten minutes from now; it's now, this moment, which will pass and be followed by more passing moments, a flow of time in which we're carried forward. Our journey is smoothed when we learn to let go, and it's eased by the joy we learn to take in "undeep and unabiding things."

Paradoxical but true: I'll find lasting happiness only when I let go of the notion of permanence.

September 24

Happiness is an endowment and not an acquisition. It depends more upon temperament and disposition than environment.
— *John J. Ingalls*

We carry within us the ingredient which assures smooth travel today, if that's our choice. In our exchanges with life, we can project an attitude of gladness or regret. We can be grateful for our blessings or resentful that we have only what we have. We can offer love to our fellow travelers or harbor envy. However, when we choose to enter a situation, a discussion perhaps, offering loving acceptance of whatever we encounter, we'll discover the prevailing inner happiness.

Becoming aware that the power to be happy is at our fingertips is profoundly exhilarating. At first it may also be frightening because we can no longer deny responsibility for our feelings. Every moment of our lives we are making a choice about how to feel.

Emotional maturity follows on the coattails of responsible choice-making. Never again must I wait for another to make me happy. It's in my power to be happy, today.

*Old things were stirring: the old illness of
remembering was going to start again.*
                    —Rosamond Lehmann

Does the act of remembering ever resemble
an illness? Yes, if it causes pain. For many of
us, memories of our past behavior seem to live
in cages, like wild animals; if we enter the cages,
the beasts attack us.

Why do we give memory this power to
wound? We sometimes seem to want the unproductive pain of a shameful remembrance,
as though we had sentenced ourselves to feel
badly, as if our pain could alter the past—or
pay for it.

It's time to forgive ourselves. We know what's
past is past, and the only time we have is the
present. We may feel as though we carry a
complicated weight of guilt and shame, but the
act of releasing ourselves is simple—an act of
self-acceptance. Let us greet the present in
the best way we know, and let go of regrets.

*I will tame my memories, so that they become my com-
panions if I choose.*

September 26

To love is to place our happiness in the happiness of another.
—*G.W. von Leibnitz*

Broadening our vision beyond our self-serving needs and acknowledging the importance of others in our lives not only lifts their spirits, but also fosters positive feelings within ourselves. Our personal happiness grows when we nourish someone else's.

That which we give to others will be given to us in time. In order to find peace, we must behave peacefully toward others. And to receive love, we must willingly and unconditionally offer it. When we try to control others' behavior, we meet resistance. We can be certain an aggressive stance invites adversity. How true is the axiom "we reap that which we sow."

My own behavior invites the treatment I'll receive today. I am free to act lovingly, respectfully, and peacefully.

But one of the attributes of love, like art, is
to bring harmony and order out of chaos.
                                        —Molly Haskell

The offer of love to the person sharing this time in our lives softens them, ourselves, and the events we share. Giving and receiving loving thoughts eases any momentary difficulty; loving and feeling loved reminds us that we are never alone in our struggles. In partnership we can survive any troubling circumstance.

Love of self, of family, of enemies increases the harmonious conditions that affect us all. Like the ripples from a pebble dropped in a stream, the act of loving moves beyond the object receiving the love at this moment. In fact, the love we give is the love we'll receive.

It is a demonstrable fact that hatred breeds hatred. Just as absolute is the knowledge that the love we offer another makes easier their gift of love to yet another. Love multiplies itself and the harmony created nurtures us all.

Love makes partners of us all. No circumstances can fell me when I'm in company with another. I will look among my associates today for willing partners.

September 28

*Honor: what a spiky, uncomfortable thing
it can be. I expect the young are wise to be
dropping it.*

—Rose Macaulay

Each generation looks at its children with
mingled pride and horror and thinks they are
destroying standards, overturning values, and
generally going to wrack and ruin. In Greece,
in the fourth century B.C., Plato complained
that young people had no morals and that their
music was barbaric.

What we've not understood, for 2500 years
and more, is that each new generation simply
re-names the old truths in the process of making
them their own. Love, courage, honesty, generosity of the spirit—these values don't change,
although they may turn up in unfamiliar shapes.

Virtues may seem spiky and uncomfortable
to young people, who need to claim their own
experience. But each generation will discover
the truth for itself. We needn't fear that the
new will destroy the old; it will simply make it
new.

*I will keep in mind that the young people of each age seek
an identity that sets them apart from their elders—without realizing that in this way, too, they resemble them.*

Even a happy life cannot be without a measure
of darkness, and the word "happiness" would
lose its meaning if it were not balanced by
sadness.

—Carl Gustav Jung

Life is full of contrasts. What we perceive or feel at this moment is often heightened by an experience we just passed through. It's the sum and substance of all experiences and our feelings about them that give meaning to any single moment.

Joy is understood only in a life where discouragement has made its mark. Our lives are recharged, even glorified by every moving experience, no matter what kind of emotion is evoked. In fact, our very existence is verified each time an encounter invites an emotional response.

When we are sad, it is because it satisfies a need to feel that way. If we accept this fact, our acceptance of every emotion grounds our lives in a serenity which embraces and transcends all our feelings.

Whatever I may feel today is cause for celebration. It's a sign of my vitality.

September 30

> *Mistakes are a fact of life.*
> *It is the response to error that counts.*
> —*Nikki Giovanni*

We're not perfect. Our mistakes are consistent with the lessons we've been assigned to learn. We strive for perfection in ourselves and sometimes we demand it of others. And when we fall short of the mark, we frequently feel that all is lost. The most important and timely lesson any of us can learn today is that doing our best is as close to perfect as we need to get.

Since falling short of the mark is the norm among us, a second lesson is to learn to accept this fact. What counts is the effort. And even with our best efforts we can't be sure of the outcome. However, the outcome will be more satisfying if we are confident that we've done all we were able to do.

Shame over mistakes, or over shortcomings in general, is certain to exaggerate and multiply the negative self-opinions that generally haunt those of us who demand perfection. And the result is even more mistakes, because our attention is diverted from the task at hand. We must believe that mistakes are the guideposts to the destination we're headed for.

All is not lost if I err today. Mistakes help me stay on course, providing I'm willing to learn from them.

October

Two birds fly past.
They are needed somewhere.

—*Robert Bly*

Our lives touch the lives of thousands of other people in ever widening circles. Every act of ours has a public dimension, even something as private as sharpening a pencil or filling a teakettle. We all are needed by everyone, and our chosen lives become a necessary part of the larger pattern woven by all other lives.

Even by becoming a recluse or a hermit, we don't leave the pattern. We may change it, so that others direct their lives in a different way with respect to our own. But this is true of all choices.

And we don't see the pattern as a whole; it's too complex, too vast for us to grasp. About the best we can hope for is the optimistic detachment that lets us see that those birds are needed. The squirrels in our attic, the ants at the picnic, the angry driver honking behind us are all needed. What can we learn from them?

Today I'll rejoice in my connectedness.

October 2

The sky changes every minute . . . on the plains side of the Divide most people have visions or go mad.
—Sandra Alcosser

Our adaptability is a constant source of amazement. We can learn to live and even thrive in such radically differing settings as a high-rise apartment in New York City and a sheep-skin hut in Mongolia. We live in deserts, glaciers, swamps; on boats, in trees, and even under-ground. We can eat almost anything that any animal eats, and a lot of other things that no animal would touch. Our instinct for survival takes expression in our marvelous ability to adapt.

Some brain scientists believe that what we call madness is an adaptation, a technique for getting what we need. It's possible that visions are adaptive, too. Extraordinary behavior ex-presses extraordinary states of mind.

We're often hard on ourselves if we catch ourselves behaving oddly—humming aloud or weeping or staring in amazement at a spot on the wall. We want to be normal; we'll suppress the odd behavior. But we should pay attention; unusual behavior often means that something's going on inside us that needs attention. Maybe we're grieving a loss, or sitting on some anger. Self-acceptance and self-love will heal us better than scoldings.

I can accept even the unusual in myself. It is only one variety of humanness.

There is nothing so moving—not even acts of love or hate—as the discovery that one is not alone.
—*Robert Ardrey*

We live in concert with others, compatibly at times and at other times not so well, but always with others. We don't always acknowledge our togetherness, but when we are moved to, we quickly sense the comforts of a shared journey. We belong to more than just our neighborhood, our families, our circle of friends. The concert that has captured us is greater, and it has a conductor with whom we travel a path as well. It's this journey that encourages us to appreciate the steps we take with others.

The whole of creation depends on the contribution of each part for its completion. Interdependently, never singly and alone, we exist. We are at one with another, and this oneness is eternal.

I may not feel our oneness today, but I will trust that it is so.

October 4

I search in these words and find nothing more than myself, caught between the grapes and the thorns.

—*Anne Sexton*

We are frequently afraid to look into ourselves, to probe our depths. We've feared that if we examined our basic motives and desires, we'd find a swamp of evil: corrupt, selfish, and full of hate. But we've learned—to our considerable relief—that those fears were unfounded. We're human, that's all; not better or worse than everyone else.

We all have particular traits that we struggle with, parts of ourselves that make us unhappy. When we're feeling down on ourselves, it may seem that we're the only person in the world with that fault. "Why am I so insecure?" "No one else talks too loud!" "I hate being so competitive." If we could see into the hearts of our friends and associates we would find virtually the same struggles.

And yet we go on fearing the monster lurking in those woods. Let's bring that specter into the light; it's only ourselves, constant traveler between pain and joy.

I only fear what I don't know; self-knowledge is my real life's work.

*My mission on earth is to recognize the void
—inside and outside of me—and fill it.*
                              —Rabbi Menahem

Emptiness often haunts us. The alienation
we feel that accompanies us to work, to parties,
even among friends, is letting us know that we
need to nurture our inner selves. Within each of
us lives the small child who feels fear, fear about
a particular outcome, or our ability to handle a
situation. As we practice caring for our inner
child in all of our experiences we'll discover a
spiritual strength and a calmness that eluded us
in the past. Consciously developing a connection
to the inner child at first lessens the brunt of
the external world, then removes it.

The spirit-child becomes our strength and
our hope when we turn to it. It fills us; it comforts us as we comfort it. We no longer doubt
our place in this life.

*If I go within today to offer comfort, I'll find it. I will not
feel alone or fearful if I reach within and take the hand
of strength.*

October 6

I was taught that the way of progress is neither swift nor easy.
—Marie Curie

Some of our goals are easily attained. Others demand stamina and resourcefulness. And still others require a commitment of long standing, a willingness to postpone gratification, but most of all, an acceptance of possible failure. We can never be certain of a final outcome. We can only be sure of our effort. However, we can be assured that honest effort will allow us to make measurable progress.

Life is a process. We learn and grow and move toward our goals little by little. The choice to quit moving is also available to us. In fact, a breather from the path we're on is occasionally in order. Recommitment is necessary, however, to begin the growth process again.

Charging ahead takes energy—emotional, mental, spiritual, even physical energy. The whole person is involved in the process of growth; our progress is in direct correlation to the process.

Today may challenge me, but I will make progress.

*The battle to keep up appearance unneces-
sarily, the mask—whatever name you give
creeping perfectionism—robs us of our
energies.*
　　　　　　　　　　　—Robin Worthington

Because we fear we're inadequate, and because our expectations of ourselves are inflated
along with our assumptions about others' expectations of us, we live in the realm of pretense.
However, the truth of existence is that we're
exactly who we need to be. None of us is inadequate, yet all of us fall short of being perfect.
Our journeys are designed to introduce us to
new information, new possibilities for growth
and development.

We must trust that we are at the right place,
at the right time, with all the preparation we
need to succeed, here and now. Fretting takes
our focus away from the moment and the rich
invitation for personal involvement that it's ex-
tending. Remember, it's through the full interaction with the present that we are nurtured
emotionally and spiritually and encouraged to
attain our full potential.

Today I'll remember that I'm all I need to be.

October 8

With nothing to do but expect the hour of setting off, the afternoon was long. . . .
— Jane Austen

The most important single determinant of how we feel at any given time is our attitude. If we live in the moment, use the moment to the full, we will never be bored and seldom depressed. The surest way to bring on a negative mood is to deny the present, whether by dwelling on the past or by fantasizing about the future.

The past is unalterable; the future, beyond our control. All we have is now, and all we can work with is our present attitude and behavior. Everything that we value, our dreams, plans, and hopes, dwindle to insignificance before the moment. How we act right now is how we are right now. If we let ourselves dodge the moment, longing for a phone call that might not come or eating a candy bar because we'll diet tomorrow, we're negating all our best intentions.

I will look to the moment, and miraculously, the future will take care of itself. If I can achieve clarity and honesty right here, today, I'll give my future a good start.

We have our brush and colors—paint Paradise and in we go.
                                    —Nikos Kazantzakis

We find in our experiences and in our daily reveries just what we anticipate. If we greet the day wearing a smile, confident that we are needed and able to make a contribution, we'll discover that the day holds great promise. What we need to understand is that every day holds just as much promise as we're capable of expecting. We carry within ourselves the image of the picture we're creating.

Since the choice to find happiness rather than sorrow and regret is our own, why does the latter even attract us? For no other reason than we fail to believe that we're deserving of happiness. We know our own shortcomings; we're aware of the details in our lives for which we feel shame. We think only the pure of heart deserve happiness. But we're human. And this means mistakes are normal and expected. With wisdom comes full understanding of this fact. In the meantime, we can trust that happiness is our birthright. All that's requested is our belief in it.

Today will offer me all that I truly desire. Happiness attracts itself.

October 10

*Imagination has always had powers of res-
urrection that no science can match.*
—Ingrid Bengis

Imagining the successful completion of a goal
increases the likelihood of its attainment.
Whether we imagine our success in an athletic
event, a college program, or preparing a meal,
the image formulates a mind-set that's con-
ducive to the goal's completion.

Seeing ourselves leap with grace to hit a high,
wide tennis shot makes the movement familiar
when we're on the court. Hearing ourselves
answer correctly a committee's queries reduces
the anxiety when the test date arrives. Every
anticipated event can be prepared for if we use
our imagination creatively. However, we need
to be aware that imagination can run wild if
we're not responsibly in the driver's seat. At no
time does someone else have the power to put
wild, fearful ideas in our minds. And yet, we're
each capable of absorbing someone else's negative suggestions if we're not actively imagining
our own positive ones.

*No day is free from some level of anxiety about an impend-
ing situation. Relief from this anxiety lies in my mind.
I'll use my imagination wisely today.*

*Woe to him that is alone when he falleth,
for he hath not another to help him up.*
                                    —Ecclesiastes

If we are stepping through this life, indifferent to those around us and thus separate from our fellow human beings, it is by conscious choice. It may be hard to reach out to someone close, but there will always be a willing hand to receive our own. Each of us has been created to offer others our unique gifts. When we choose a posture of indifference, we are denying to the universe what we have to give.

There is magic in the realization that our acquaintances, our co-workers and neighbors, are presented to us by design. We are here to learn lessons and we play teacher to each other. When we have stepped away from the circle of people calling to us, we are denying them the opportunities for growth they may need and preventing it in ourselves as well. We need one another and being helped by someone else fulfills more needs than our own.

We are in one another's world by design. I will enjoy the magic of that meaning, today.

October 12

Nobody can hurt you but yourself. Every experience you have makes you all the more fit for life.

—"Box-Car Bertha"

We commonly say, "She hurt me," or "I'm afraid of hurting him." Yet no one can hurt us without our cooperation. Other people's actions don't affect us, unless we choose to let them; and no words can wound unless we turn them into weapons.

Some of what we call hurt is really learning. Because our pride may stiffen us against change, especially when we're young, any learning that brings about a change in our behavior will hurt. As we learn humility, we bend more easily. And we learn not to accept pain from others.

All experience teaches us something, if we'll learn. There will be pain along with wisdom; perhaps the price of wisdom is pain. But everything we learn enhances our life.

I'll come to understand my pain and find its value for my life.

Every physician almost hath his favorite disease.

—Henry Fielding

We wouldn't go to a dentist for corns or bunions, just as we wouldn't go looking for fresh fruit at a hardware store. By and large, we know where to go for what we want. Why is it, then, that sometimes we persist in asking something from one who cannot give it?

We recognize unreasonable demands when we meet them, but not always when we make them. Parents expect mature judgment from young children; children expect saintly patience or flexibility from their parents. Commonly, we expect our friends or lovers to show us their loyalty and affection without our asking.

Reality teaches us that if we want something, we should go to a likely source, and ask for what we want. If we're not willing to ask, we'll have to settle for every physician's favorite treatment—whether or not we have the disease.

Today I'll remember to ask for what I want from an appropriate source.

October 14

Every human being has, like Socrates, an attendant spirit; and wise are they who obey its signals.

—Lydia M. Child

At no instant are we honestly at a loss about what steps to take, what decision to make. Each of us is both guarded and guided by an inner voice that we occasionally tune in on, but more frequently tune out. We may have defined the inner voice as conscience. However, it's not important what we think it is; it's only important that we acknowledge it. The inner voice is our special connection to the spiritual realm, a network that links us all, whether we acknowledge it or not.

The choice to listen to the inner message is a ready option, and it will never fail to benefit us. As we familiarize ourselves with it, and trust it enough to act as directed, we'll glory in both the comfort and the sureness of the action we take. We sense that we're not alone. Even when no other human is present, we're not alone. Always we are connected to the spirit-energy that inspires us all to right action.

Every dreaded circumstance is made easier if I'm accustomed to going within for guidance. Today can run as smoothly as I want. I'll seek my inner voice.

No man is an island entire of itself. Each is
a piece of the continent, a part of the main.
—John Donne

Our problems seem so singular; we often
feel alone with our struggles. And it's true that
each of us must come to our own terms with
whatever situation faces us. But no struggle
facing us is free from the influence of other
people and their struggles. We have a shared
destiny which is accompanied by individual perceptions and both singular and mutual responses to the ebb and flow enfolding us all.

Knowing that we share this journey offers
comfort when we need it in our daily struggles.
We are not alone, forgotten, unimportant to the
destiny of others. Nor are others without meaning in the experiences we're gifted with. Our
existences are mutual—we are interdependent
contributors to the total life cycle.

What each of us learns eases the struggles of
another. All experiences are meant for the good
of us all.

Today I may feel alone, but I'm not. My life is fully in
concert with those around me, and all is as it should be.

October 16

. . . it wasn't sin that was born on the day when Eve picked an apple: what was born on that day was a splendid virtue called disobedience.

—Oriana Fallaci

Liberty of conscience is precious to us. We need to feel that we are doing the right thing; sometimes, this may mean disobeying authority, as abolitionists, suffragists, and conscientious objectors have done.

Yet when we search our hearts, it is our own authority, or the authority of a spiritual source outside ourselves, that commands our true loyalty. And others must trust this authority, for themselves. Trust in ourselves teaches us to be respectful of others' beliefs.

Obedience must be based on trust. If this is true for us, we can understand that it's equally true for others. Our spirit is larger than our beliefs, and more generous.

Today I'll try to understand that everyone wishes to do what is right for themselves.

*Always I've found resisting temptation easier
than yielding—it's more practical and requires no initiative.*
                                    —Alice B. Toklas

If a temptation is easy to set aside, it can't
tempt us very strongly. The real, insidious
temptations are the ones to which we yield un-
thinkingly: temptations to inertia, for example,
or to stinginess or self-punishment.

It's part of our puritan heritage that makes us
equate "temptation" with "indulgence." We're
armed against sensuous indulgence; we can be
strong in resisting a casual romance, a piece of
pecan pie, or an extra hour's sleep. We don't
feel tempted by the small meannesses that nib-
ble away at our souls, and therefore we yield
without examining alternatives.

Can we learn to recognize these little temptations to anger, to a closed heart? Can we learn
to see the feelings that we're tempted to suppress—feelings of love, pity, or communion
with others—as occasions for spiritual growth
and deliverance?

*I needn't deprive myself of joy. Learning to recognize what
tempts me to joylessness will help me to develop my spiritual
wealth.*

October 18

Some day science may have the existence of mankind in its power, and the human race (may) commit suicide by blowing up the world.

—Henry Adams

One hundred years ago, Henry Adams foresaw the plight we're in today. Some observers believe that people in positions of power won't be able to refrain from the awful destruction of a nuclear war.

If we believe that the glory of the human spirit is our ability to choose our future, it's important for us to refuse to agree. We must do everything we can to prevent this murderous suicide of our species, and the first thing we must do is to choose to leave war behind us. Our slow progress on this planet, from naked apes to technicians in clothing, has prepared us to make the noble choice of peace. We owe it to our humanity.

Among those who despair of our capacity to make this choice are people with brilliant intellects. They may not, however, be our wisest counselors. Each of us must listen to the truth within our hearts; there lies the wisdom that we need. Let's not confuse war with patriotism; we're all citizens of the whole world, and war hurts our human family.

When my spirit is tranquil, I can listen to the peace in my heart.

*The evening star
is the most
beautiful of all stars.*

—*Sappho*

The first star in the evening sky shines with a special brightness, because it is the first. We see it as a signal; the first sign that afternoon has turned to evening.

The first of anything is touched with special glamour; first love, a baby's first words or steps, first day of school, first job. They're signals of change, profound and irreversible. When day turns to evening, that day will never come again. Tomorrow is a new day, unique and never-to-be-repeated.

If we could meet each new day, each new person, each new experience, as though it were the first, our lives could be touched by the excitement and discovery of adventure. We're not the same as we were yesterday. Each moment we change; each new event in our lives can be a cusp between two different states. Today, let's give ourselves that special gift.

Each moment is the first of a new series. I will be attentive.

October 20

. . . What is in one's life stays there to the end
of one's days.
                                        —*Harrison Salisbury*

Young people often try to pretend they're
other than they truly are; they're pleased to be
taken for natives in a strange place, or tourists
at home. People try to change their hair color,
their body shape, or their voice; trying on identities, escaping from themselves.

It's natural to play around with external signs
of who we are. We all look for a style that will let
us express who we want to be. But we're indel-
ibly marked, by our genes and our upbringing.
We're made so that virtually nothing we've ever
cared about is lost to us. Although we can choose
our behavior, we can't choose our antecedents.

We may rail against this in our youth, but
by middle age, most of us will be glad for it. One
secret of happiness is liking who we are. And
that's where our power to choose is important:
since we can't change who we are, we gracefully
choose to be the best possible us.

I shall be grateful for this day, in which I can make the
most of what I have.

*Humor is such a strong weapon, such a strong
answer.*

—*Agnes Varda*

We take life so seriously, certain that the
situation confronting us, or at least the next
one, will doom us. We gravely anticipate what
lies ahead and assuredly we'll experience what
we expect. The power to lighten our load rests
within. We're only a decision away from an
easier life, one that's built with laughter rather
than perpetual gloom.

Few of us are aware of the therapeutic effects
of laughter. As Norman Cousins demonstrated
in his battle with cancer, laughter can activate
our total being, recharging the whole system.
Besides the positive visceral effects, laughter
grants a balanced perspective in life that encourages greater emotional health. Laughing at
our human foibles takes away their sting, reduc-
ing them to minor irritants, the kind that are
easily forgotten when we've developed a healthier perspective.

Nothing has power over us except by our
consent. No problem, no difficult person assumes command unless we've abdicated our
own position of power. Remember the strength
laughter lends us when a situation gets snarled.

*Every situation has a humorous interpretation. My day
will be lengthened if I look for reasons to laugh. Without
fail, they are present.*

October 22

> *If you want knowledge, you must take part in
> the practice of changing reality. If you want to
> know the taste of a pear, you must change
> the pear by eating it yourself.*
> —Mao Tse-tung

Our language is poor in words that convey
emotional meaning. To know, for instance, with
the intellect, is not the same as knowing with all
our being. We can "know" in our heads that
the universe is infinite, but until we experience
that knowledge in our hearts, our spirits, in the
pit of our stomachs—we can't really know it.

Full knowledge means change. Experience of
the infinite changes us; once we have experienced awe, we are not the same. We can understand oppression or injustice, but until we experience it in our bones and breath, the knowledge
is not truly available to us.

The knowledge that changes is the knowledge
we seek. And sometimes we must change in
order to obtain it. If we find ourselves living in
a way that contradicts what we know, we
change our lives.

We are continually changing as we grow.
Our spiritual progress is a record of small
changes that bring us closer to the truth our
spirit recognizes.

*I will not fear change; I will trust that it brings the knowl-
edge I need.*

*To wait for someone else, or to expect someone
else to make my life richer, or fuller, or more
satisfying, puts me in a constant state of
suspension.*
—*Kathleen Tierney Andrus*

How tempting it is to make another person
responsible for our happiness, and how absurd.
To give such power to others means we're at
their mercy; it does not mean we're happy.
Whereas, accepting full responsibility for our
own acts and feelings does give us the power to
be as happy as we choose, as often as we choose.

Emotional maturity precludes our blaming or
praising another for our personal well-being.
There is reason to be exhilarated that we are
blessed with as much control as we choose to
have over our own growth, happiness, and commitment to change. We're in another's control
only by choice—never by necessity. And when
we've given our precious power away, we're
reduced to waiting—waiting for someone else's
nod of approval, waiting for their invitation to
live.

*The time is now to decide for myself who I am, where I'm
going, and why! The time is now.*

October 24

*The true use of speech is not so much to express
our wants as to conceal them.*
                                    —Oliver Goldsmith

Learning to communicate, for little children,
means squeezing huge desires into little words,
like "hurt" or "cookie." We learn early that we're
only going to get part of what we want.

Some of us never recover from this disappointment. We use words to manipulate others,
to hide our feelings. We may imagine that we
have the power to control others, and so we tell
ingenious stories to mask what we think is our
naked strength.

But we're deluding ourselves, rather than
other people. The strategy of falsehood and
control finally traps us in a web of lies, where
even we don't know what we want. Clarity is
a choice, and so is happiness, if we want to
choose them.

*Asking for something is risky: I might be refused. But
if I don't even ask, I'll never hear "yes."*

The game of life is a game of boomerangs.
Our thoughts, deeds, and words return to us
sooner or later, with astounding accuracy.
                                        —Florence Scovel Shinn

We plant the seeds of the bounty we'll reap by every action we take. We teach others how to treat us by our treatment of them coupled with our own level of self-respect. Never should we be surprised at the level of comfort or discomfort we experience in our interactions with others. We have invited it.

Fortunately, we are in control of our own behavior, which means we have the choice to act responsibly and with respect for others every moment of our lives. We can be certain that we'll be treated in similar fashion throughout the day. The terms of life are simple when defined in this way. We get what's our due—and we've prearranged it ourselves.

It's seldom that circumstances discourage us as much as our relations with others. Most often our frustrations or depression are people-centered. The good news is that we have the capability to favorably influence all outcomes that involve other persons. At every opportunity, remember the treatment we each desire and offer that to others.

I am in command of my behavior today. It will invite similar reaction. I'll put my best foot forward.

October 26

Though the seas threaten, they are merciful,
I have cursed them without cause.
                    —William Shakespeare

To each of us, our own self is the most important person in the world. I am the only person who can get what I want; you are the only person who can make you happy or unhappy. This doesn't mean that the world revolves around us, though.

When we were infants, we believed it did. We valued things according to how they affected us. A rainstorm was good if it meant we didn't have to visit relatives who bored us, but it was bad if it spoiled a picnic. We took everything personally.

It's not easy to give up being the center of the universe; some of us cling to the notion long after we've given up bottles and diapers. But once we acknowledge the impersonality of most events, we can stop taking responsibility for the weather, Soviet foreign policy, the outcome of labor negotiations. We can even stop taking other people's actions personally. Other people don't really get sick of us, succeed or fail for our benefit, or live or die because of us. It's wonderful to take the pressure off.

The only thing I need to take personally is my person.

The sun, the hero of every day, the impersonal old man that beams as brightly on death as on birth, came up every morning. . . .
—*Zora Neale Hurston*

Details bog us down. When we count the trees, we never breathe in the forest. Keeping our focus close means escaping the wider ranges of perception and robbing ourselves of the chance to see more than one little slice of life.

When we're children, everything is near and far at the same time. So many things are new that we need to anchor our perceptions with small bits of the familiar: security blankets, familiar toys, a well-loved thumb.

Grown-ups presumably learn to do without these "transitional objects." Yet we need some certainties in a life of shifting priorities and relative values. We're lucky if we can find our anchor within ourselves. We are the real heroes of every day; we come up every morning out of the individual details of our sleeping minds, and it's given to us to shine brightly on the events that touch us, whatever they may be.

Today may I find both zest in living and detachment from the petty details of life.

October 28

> *. . . my work was so long so little appreciated that I learned not to care a scrap for either blame or praise.*
>
> —*James Murray*

It's instructive to look at important figures of the past. So many have fallen into utter obscurity, and people who were quite obscure are now seen as important. Who remembers newspaper columnists or best-selling writers of forty years ago? Yet at the time, their names were on everyone's lips.

We have an idea that life has speeded up, that history has accelerated, in that we live faster now than people did in the past. But this is a function of the media; the experiences we hear about are other people's experiences. We know more, sooner, about more people; we know when royal babies are born and when border wars are fought. But these events have always occurred, and have always totally engrossed those who are immediately concerned. Their true import for the world, history must discover.

When we have a staunch purpose, it's possible to ignore the praise or blame of those we don't care about. Whereas people who bloom early may be early sidetracked, the pace of our own lives is under our direction; so is our real significance in the lives of others.

Obscurity can be a blessing. It will never warp my values.

*I think that most of us become self-critical
as soon as we become self-conscious.*
                                    —Ellen Goodman

It seems all too common that we reject our own best efforts as not good enough. Few of us are satisfied with anything less than perfection in ourselves or others. Criticism is second nature to us, and it does an injustice to both giver and receiver.

The self-image of all humanity could stand a lift. Negativity has gained a strong foothold in our minds, and it digs its talons deeper with every barb given or received. Fortunately, we have the individual and collective power to change our thoughts and the direction we are heading, as individuals and in concert with others. Being positive toward ourselves and others wields great power. Positive strokes encourage greater efforts which guarantee positive results.

I can be self-critical or self-congratulating today. My choice will determine the day's success.

October 30

Who would care to question the ground of forgiveness or compassion?
— *Joseph Conrad*

Some people don't seem able to accept the things that come to them; they always want to go back and dwell on how it was before and what mistakes were made by them and others. Sometimes they want to prove, by this recital of past errors, that they were right; sometimes they seem to want to dwell on their own fallibility.

We can't make much progress toward serenity of the spirit without reconciling the past. If old wounds or conflicts rankle, we need to accept them, forgive them, and let them go. Above all, let's forgive ourselves. Those past errors turned into valuable lessons, didn't they? Life is too short to hold grudges, and they take up energy and time that we could use for spiritual growth.

Each day is new, and this new day is all of time for us, right now. This day can flow pure and clear or we can choke it with old grudges, regrets, or fears—the choice is ours.

The ground of forgiveness and compassion is fertile ground; from it comes my harvest of the future.

Adventure is something you seek for pleasure,
. . . but experience is what really happens to
you in the long run; the truth that finally
overtakes you.
— *Katherine Anne Porter*

In our search for new thrills, for unfamiliar ventures, we will become privy to situations and experiences designed for our personal growth. Our desires to chart new courses, to travel untrammeled paths are consistent with the inner source of truth and knowledge that subtly and gracefully guides our movements.

Whatever the occurrences in our lives, the circumstances we'd rather shun as well as those that absorb us, we can relish the knowledge that they've sought us out to introduce us to new levels of truth. We can be secure that what we need to learn, we'll be taught. The experiences promising the opportunities needed to fulfill our personal potential will be present today and the days ahead.

I will trust today's experiences, secure in the knowledge that they are meant for me, at this time.

November

Order is a lovely thing;
On disarray it lays its wing,
Teaching simplicity to sing.
                    —Anna Hempstead Branch

Things and events have their own order. It's human to want to impose order from the outside—our order; but often, our attempt to put things in order resembles the old man who tried to push the river. It never went any faster, and if he stopped pushing, it got there just the same.

Some people seem to have a knack for order. It could be that they've learned to let things take their own shape. If order is natural, then maybe disorder is what we create with our human fussing. It could be, too, that disorder is in the eye of the beholder—especially if the beholder is a perfectionist.

Serenity is the ability to appreciate natural order.

Today I'll try to be light on my feet and get out of my own way.

November 2

Putting a question correctly is one thing and finding the answer to it is something quite different.

— *Anton Chekhov*

Questions and answers lie within us. Unfortunately, they don't come in matched sets, numbered or color-keyed so we can match them up. Sometimes we think we have all the answers and we wish we knew the questions.

In fact, the questions are often more difficult to find, especially questions that have to do with our deepest feelings. What do we want? How do we feel about it? Such questions threaten to expose us—to lay bare our vulnerable selves.

For once we acknowledge that we want something, we risk not getting it. But if we can remain deaf even to question, we protect our vulnerability. The other side of that, of course, is that we'll never get what we want until we acknowledge that question. We must work to choose the risk of hearing the wrong answer over the certainty of deafness.

Is lack of pain worth shutting down my capacity for pleasure? Let me strengthen myself to risk joy.

November 3

*Getting started can be very hard for people
who have trouble with beginnings. After all,
where do beginnings begin?*
                              —Dorothy Bryant

Most of us have trouble getting started at one
time or another. It's a common phenomenon,
whether the project is Christmas cookies, an
annual report, or cleaning the attic: "I just don't
know where to begin."

It's a good rule to begin with ourselves, in the
moment that is. Start the project where we are
now. The other things that are necessary—
details from the past and plans for the future—
will reveal themselves as the project takes shape.

Sometimes we will begin, like writers, by
talking about how hard it is to begin. This seems
to oil the wheels; they start to turn, and before
we know it, we've begun (though we may have
to throw away the first paragraph).

*Trying to begin "at the beginning" is a good way to drive
myself mad. I will grasp the tools that are at hand: myself
and the moment.*

November 4

Together is a road travelled by the brave.
— *George Betts*

Moving through life fully in concert with others requires commitment and much energy. It demands self-love, unconditional acceptance of others, patience, the ability to be vulnerable and to take risks, and the decision to stay put even when the desire to run is great. And this assortment of characteristics is only the beginning. More is required of us, much more, if we want a real experience of belonging to those around us. But even more than that is guaranteed for us if we are willing to *be present always*.

If we've chosen to go it alone in the past, we can quickly recall the frequent uncertainty, the defensiveness when questioned by others, the absence of emotional support when the going was rough. But then, we may have believed we were free—others didn't have to be counted on. However, real freedom to be who we are can only be found among a circle of friends who have committed themselves to us, just as we've committed ourselves likewise.

Together we'll grow, find happiness, and gain strength.

I will lock arms today and move forward in the company of those who need me. I need them also.

*We have a tradition in my family: We wash
our own laundry, we raise our own children,
and we clean up our own dirt.*
                                    —Alice Silverman

One life is all we have, and it's enough. One
life contains plenty of joy, sorrow, exaltation,
despair, astonishment, and cruelty. Why then
do we borrow trouble? Every time we take
responsibility for someone else's deeds, whether
they're failures or successes, we're borrowing
trouble—just as we rob ourselves when we
refuse to take responsibility for our own.

Somehow we learn to give away our powers
of independent choice. Somewhere we learned
to say, "You make me miserable," and "Look
what you made me do." But we can unlearn
these twisted borrowings; we can learn to stand
straight, be ourselves, and own our own lives.
The power to be happy or miserable lies within
us; when we give away our power to choose, we
should be very sure we know what we're getting
in return.

*If I feel trapped, let me look at how I built the trap, and
how I can take it apart. Where I used to say, "I can't,"
let me practice saying, "I won't."*

November 6

> *The nature of consciousness is to flow. It seems ever changing. States of mind succeed one another. . . . We can direct consciousness to an idea or impulse, but we cannot lock it in place.*
> —Dr. George Weinberg

Our minds are marvelous, always moving, growing, absorbing, discarding, storing. And we are in control of the direction our minds take. Thus, it's by choice, either conscious or unconscious, that we dwell on negative outcomes rather than positive projections.

Claiming ownership of and responsibility for the direction of our minds and our lives develops a sense of individual power and, in turn, enhances self-esteem. *We are what we think.* We can think ourselves into becoming better selves.

We are free, at last, from the overwhelming feelings of powerlessness and impotence. The decision to take control of our thoughts and attitudes will be the turning point. When we complement that decision by offering positive direction to our minds, we'll quickly benefit from the advantageous outcomes.

I will utilize my personal power today. I will believe in positive outcomes. I will have hope.

*There are two ways of spreading light: to be
the candle or the mirror that receives it.*
— *Edith Wharton*

Each of us carries within us the power to
illuminate others. Likewise, we are enlightened
by others' gifts of perception. Every exchange
of ideas, each expression of feeling instructs us
when our restraints against new information
are broken down.

It is an awesome realization that whoever and
whatever engages us is purposeful, having its
place in our development at the moment. Nothing is for naught, and what we are inspired to
share with another, too, fits into their scheme.

There is a message to be gleaned every moment. The choice to be enlightened awaits us.

*Today will offer me lessons and information that I need.
Will I accept enlightenment?*

November 8

The most blessed thing in the world is to live
by faith without imputation of guilt; having
the kingdom within.

—*Paul Goodman*

What does it mean, to have the kingdom within? At those times when we're happiest, we also
feel most blessed. The kingdom is one name for
a peaceful spirit.

There are times, though, when we doubt
whether anyone could live this way, in hope
and joy. No regrets, no fears, no guilty conscience; how can it be? So often we feel we have
to cover our happiness with misery; to feel bad
in order to feel good. But the inner kingdom is
built of self-acceptance. When we learn to love
ourselves for the good people we are, that kingdom is ours.

Even when happiness is not our condition,
even when sadness clouds our lives, we can be
peaceful. By knowing ourselves to be good, and
by believing we deserve goodness in return, we
will acquire the strength to endure. The faith
we live by is a peaceful, hopeful faith in the
goodness of our spirit.

I'll work to free myself from the shadow of old shame
and guilt. I can be as blessed as I choose to become.

*I was to give a child security and tenderness,
but didn't feel I received enough of this myself.*
                              —Liv Ullman

We can increase our level of serenity by learning to nurture ourselves. The child in us continues to need security and tenderness, even
while other children in our lives may call on our
reserves. We can ask for nurturing from others,
but our surest source is ourselves.

People who have never learned to love themselves may not be able to tap their source of
security and tenderness. It's never too late to
start loving ourselves, fortunately. Neglect and
abuse in early life may have damaged us; we may
have to unlearn many years of mistaken lessons.
What better time than the present?

Self-nurturing is a great adventure. We must
remember to have patience with ourselves, for
deep trust and security, the kind we all need,
don't happen in a moment. Especially if we're
unlearning some damage, we must go slowly.
We are a precious gift, to ourselves and others,
and we deserve love and nurture.

*Today I will love myself, and patiently care for my needs
so that my security soon will grow to include others.*

November 10

> *To be what we are, and to become what we are*
> *capable of becoming is the only end of life.*
> —*Robert Louis Stevenson*

Our creation was our invitation to contribute that which is uniquely our own to the life process. Our brothers and sisters have been likewise invited. Our experiences are not without purpose. They offer us opportunities to practice the contributions we have been created to make.

Realizing potential is possible when we are committed to stepping forward to meet the challenges head on. No challenge is beyond our capability; every challenge promises new growth and a measure of serenity. Our search for security, for self-worth, if it's sincere, pledges us to stay with the daily challenges. They will teach us all that we are prepared to learn.

I go forth today with anticipation and gratitude for the opportunities to be wholly one. My experiences will be exactly what I'm ready for.

Miracles do not happen.
                    —*Mathew Arnold*

Many of us will insist that miracles *do* happen. We've seen transformations in ourselves or our loved ones that have seemed miraculous, strokes of fate, demonstrations of divine intervention.

Yet, we must do our part. If we look at the history of our personal miracles, we can usually see that time, pain, and patience prepared the way. Nothing comes from nothing. The changes that transform our lives are born from the suffering that is itself a reason for change.

Whether or not we believe that a higher power intervenes directly in this world's affairs, we realize, if we think about it, that humans must be ready. To catch a falling star, we must be standing under it.

Today I'll try to position myself in readiness for whatever miracle might come my way.

November 12

> *. . . the function of freedom is to free somebody else.*
>
> —*Toni Morrison*

We all struggle over the issue of freedom—how much we want; how much we're comfortable with; how able we are to accept others' freedom. We cannot grow and create unless free to do so; in fact, our progress will be proportional to the freedom we feel to breathe, to move, to live fully.

Control is the opposite of freedom. It steals the freedom of the controller as well as the one controlled. No one grows emotionally, intellectually, or spiritually if energy is being expended controlling. And yet, the human condition is such that we passively, if not willingly, practice the game of control with the many principal characters in our lives. It's a game no one wins. Even when we're seemingly in control we lose our freedom, too, when our attention is given over to the control of someone else.

No one is free until we are all free, and, when free, we will find joy in our work, at home, and with friends. We too will discover the measure of joy we encourage others to experience.

If I reach out to love, I'll find love. If I mete out control, I'll be diminished in turn.

November 13

*God's most lordly gift to man is decency of
mind.*

—*Aeschylus*

"Decent" means appropriate, proper, becoming. Decency of mind means to think appropriate thoughts, to respond properly to events and
people, neither exaggerating nor trivializing
their importance. What a consolation it must
be to have a mind always in balance, always
ready to dwell on the good and let the negative
aspects go!

It's possible to achieve such decency. Perhaps
it is a gift from a higher power; but we must
ready ourselves to receive a gift like that. Becoming ready for the gift of a balanced outlook
entails work: the work of overcoming our ten-
dencies to, on the one hand, ignore, postpone,
and forget unpleasantness, and on the other, to
dwell on misfortune until we let it blot out the
sun.

Decency is another name for the middle way,
the true road. When we achieve decency of
mind, we'll know it by the serenity of our outlook. Obstacles won't melt, but they will assume
their true proportions.

Today I'll ready myself to receive the gift of a decent mind.

November 14

> *In soloing—as in other activities—it is far easier to start something than it is to finish it.*
>
> —Amelia Earhart

Our inspiration to master any art, to attain any goal, to tackle any project comes from within—the center of all knowledge. All of us are gifted with all knowledge. When the desire to pursue a particular avenue keeps presenting itself, we should pay heed, trusting that we will be shown the way to succeed. This desire is our invitation to develop our talents in ways that may even be foreign to our conscious minds.

The decision to trust the desire is only the first step in tackling a new project. What comes after is effort and daily recommitment to completion of the goal or project. It is much easier to switch goals or projects than to see them to their end, but it's in their doing that we develop our talents to their fullest. Each time we back off, letting our commitment die, we are opting for less than a full life. No one else can handle a project in just our way.

Today I'll be faced with the choice to stay on top of my goals. I must remember the source of my inspiration and trust it.

November 15

*To be happy means to be free, not from pain
or fear, but from care or anxiety.*
                                    —W.H. Auden

The ancient meaning of "happy" comes from "hap," or chance—as in mis-hap, or hap-pening. Happy meant fortunate or lucky, and we still call people happy who manage to turn life's unpredictability to their advantage.

Could happiness be a matter of attitude? If we persist in calling our cups half full instead of half empty, if we re-value setbacks as opportunities, aren't we behaving happily? Happiness of attitude is like a muscle: use strengthens it. Whatever *happens* to us, we should be determined to meet it positively.

Happiness can't protect us from life's woes, but it can ensure that we won't double those woes by worry or regret. We can't control other people or events; all we're responsible for is our own behavior. The decision to behave happily could change our life.

Anxiety shuts me in. I'll let it go and be free to respond happily to whatever comes.

November 16

> *Continuous effort—not strength or intelligence—is the key to unlocking our potential.*
> —Liane Cordes

Perseverance is the plus that assures us of goal completion. Unquestionably, every one of us is capable of achievement. All that's required is that we commit ourselves with determination to the task before us, one moment at a time, one day at a time. Our rewards will be many. Among them will be accomplished goals, high self-esteem and a secure sense of well-being.

It's probable that we sometimes fail to recognize our worth or understand the real value of our talents. It's likely too that on occasion we shut out of our consciousness the knowledge that our very existence validates our necessity to the whole of creation. Self-reminders are important. They're like vitamins; they contribute to our nourishment.

When we have lost sight of our ability to make valuable contributions to society, we slow down our efforts. We close ourselves off from others and our potential is stifled. To move forward once again requires only our attention to the moment engulfing us. We can handle what lies before us.

Today my efforts are needed, in the here and now. That's all.

. . . be patient toward all that is unsolved
in your heart and try to love the questions
themselves like locked rooms and like books
that are written in a very foreign tongue.
                              —Rainer Maria Rilke

We strive to know ourselves, yet we all have
unsolved questions in our hearts. We don't need
to answer them to achieve self-understanding;
all we need do is accept them and understand
ourselves as creatures with questioning hearts.

When we're ready to receive it, the answer
will come within our grasp. Perhaps a lot of
work will be required of us: as much as learning
a foreign tongue. Or perhaps the answer will be
as simple as a key that fits the door of a locked
room. But no effort will get it until we're ready.

Patience seems like such a dull virtue, especially when we're young and eager for accomplishment. But patience is another name for
love. If we're patient with ourselves, it's because
we've achieved self-acceptance, and because we
trust that, when we need it, the secret language
and the locked room will be open to us.

I know I need not fear whatever lies hidden in my heart.

November 18

> *One is happy as the result of one's own efforts.*
>
> —George Sand

Our attitude about our circumstances or our hopes determines the tenor of a moment, eventually of the whole day.

No attitude, no feeling or emotion is foisted upon us. We have always made the choice. Perhaps our passivity regarding choices has all too often eased us into situations detrimental to our emotional health. Nevertheless, responsibility for the pain that accompanies poor choice is always our own. Conversely, the joy that is ushered in by certain other choices is also our responsibility.

Personal power commands our lives, and the fruits are as bountiful as are our choices, selectively made. We will be as happy as our choices make us, and as we decide to be.

Today is all mine, and whatever I make of it is by personal choice.

When we are no longer children, we are already dead.

　　　　　　　—*Konstantin Brancusi*

Children are born into a world whose rules they must learn. As part of the learning process, children always question rules. For simplicity's sake, we stop questioning most rules. We'll walk on sidewalks, eat with forks, talk in sentences, and keep our clothes buttoned. But the child inside us looks out with eager eyes and stands ready to question any rule that seems absurd.

Sometimes we bully that interior child into silence, for its questions embarrass us. Sometimes we hide it, sit on it, punish it—but it's always there. If we put that child to sleep, we lose one of the best parts of ourselves. We are right to question, to want to see for ourselves, especially when we're asked to do something that troubles our conscience. The child needn't always have its way, but it deserves our love. It was a young child in the crowd of people who said, "But the emperor is naked!"

I will love and nurture the child within me, and I will heed its questions, which may bring me to new answers.

November 20

*Death, when it approaches, ought not to take
one by surprise. It should be part of the full
expectancy of life.*

—*Muriel Spark*

The process of living includes many dimensions. We can joyfully anticipate high periods and we must expect pain. We won't escape sorrow over wrongs we've committed nor grief for the departure of a dear one. Anxiety over what may transpire is a given. But working to develop a balanced perception of all the events of our lives will ease our way. It's our overreactions to the ups and downs that make all of our daily steps uncertain.

Fearing the unknown wastes our time. How much better to trust that life will offer us exactly what we need to develop as healthy human beings. No event will be more than we can handle. *All* events are necessities of life, and each event needs simple acceptance.

*If I understand that every situation carries a blessing,
today will offer me comfort, throughout.*

Life is a battle in which we fall from wounds
we receive in running away.
                                    —William L. Sullivan

Our experience in this life is a composite of many lessons—lessons which will ease our personal growth and offer us the opportunities necessary to encourage our unique contributions. Clearly, not all lessons are easy or pleasurable when we first encounter them, but their rewards are great if we choose to learn from them, and we can be certain that no lesson is without its reward.

Those things we need to experience, to learn, to understand, will present themselves again and again until we have attended to them. We may choose to close our minds one time, and even close them again, but the lesson will not be put off for long. Another experience will surround us, offering once again the opportunity necessary for the personal growth we're destined to realize.

We must trust that our lives are unfolding in ways that will evoke our full potential, and that no challenge comes that earlier lessons haven't prepared us for.

Tackling my lessons head-on is a decision I can make today.

November 22

We cannot fail to meet the same problems as did our forefathers, and learning their answers may help us to act upon them as intelligently as they did, and may even, perhaps, teach us to avoid making always the same mistakes.

—Anne Fremantle

As youth, we are impatient and don't always believe in the value of elders' experience. A few mistakes, however, and most of us will acknowledge that we can learn something from the wisdom of the past.

As parents, we want to protect our children from suffering the same pain we have gone through. We may have forgotten that some risks are healthy. Fear teaches only more fear. We must experience some failure and some pain if we are to grow and learn.

The balance between safety and exploration isn't easy to strike, but everyone needs to find it. If we listen to the stillness within, we'll discover what is right for us to do—when to hang on and when to let go. We will be able to trust ourselves in both caution and bravery, and we will learn from history all it can teach us. The choices in our lives are ours to make.

If I am patient, I can understand and use the experience of others.

*A man that studieth revenge keeps his own
wounds green.*
—*Francis Bacon*

Our progress along the path of human
growth is measurable by the exercise we encourage of our forgiving spirit. Each time we
harbor a resentment toward another we block
our own growth.

Preoccupation with a troublesome situation
or person prevents our responding to the thrill
and possibilities of the moment. Stepping out
of the flow of events to stay stuck on an old
hurt guarantees us a stifled existence. Forgiveness of self and others frees us, frees our spirit
to soar ahead. And we'll do so with a glad heart.

The act of forgiveness lightens whatever
burden we may be carrying. Forgiveness heals
the soul; it energizes the spirit. It makes possible our forward movement once again.

*My hope for a good life is proportionate to my forgiving
heart. Happiness is within my power.*

November 24

> *Life is not always what one wants it to be,*
> *but to make the best of it as it is, is the only*
> *way of being happy.*
> — *Jennie Jerome Churchill*

The posture we take while performing our tasks today, and the attitude we project toward those who cross our path, will emphatically influence what the day brings. No one else can decide for any one of us what we'll feel or think about the day. We have the power to be as content, or as discontent as we make up our minds to be.

A sign of maturity is acceptance of the full responsibility for the failures as well as the successes of a day. Another sign is the willingness to let go of the day's outcomes, whatever they are, and ready ourselves instead to face tomorrow, confident and hopeful. Carrying yesterday's baggage into today will only distort the size and shape of any bundle we must handle in the twenty-four hours ahead.

I begin the day free of yesterday, unburdened, hopeful, cheerful, confident if I so choose.

Some people are so fond of ill-luck that they run half-way to meet it.
      —*Douglas William Jerrold*

It's not wholly true in this world that we make our own luck, but we certainly have a share in it. Opportunity shakes out pretty evenly for most people, but what we do with it, whether we're willing or able to grasp a chance when we see one, is an individual matter. Some of us even have trouble seeing opportunities for growth.

When we feel abused or resentful, we need to examine our own part. Have we so mistrusted our own powers that we've not let ourselves see the chances life has dealt us? It's important for us to recognize that we have a choice. If we're dissatisfied, we can choose to change. We can also choose not to change, and to complain about being stuck; but we should realize the choice is our own.

If we've had a long string of bad luck, maybe we need to look at what we're doing. If our self-esteem is very low, we may want to punish ourselves somehow, to prove that we're no good. The knowledge that we're lovable and necessary people may have slipped away, and we may need to do some structural repair. But that's okay; we're worth the effort.

I deserve to be happy and I know how—whether I'm using the knowledge or not.

November 26

*It is not until our own hearts are pierced that
we can begin to know the suffering.*
—Sarah Minturn Sedgewick

Our own painful experiences serve a worthy purpose. They make possible our understanding of another's pain. In turn, we are able healers to one another because we have shared the experience of pain.

Being present to another's sorrow or suffering is like a healing balm, lessening the burden, the intensity of pain. However, healing is only possible after the pain has been acknowledged, internally embraced, and then released by the injured person.

Frequently, we seek freedom from all pain. But pain stretches us, pushes us to grow, to develop new levels of ourselves. Pain promises us unexpected pleasure. It also requires patience of us. We have many lessons to learn in life, and each one is generally punctuated by a stab of pain. It's within our power to rejoice even when the pain is felt. It isn't without purpose.

The pain I may experience today can teach me and heal me, if I allow it to.

Living well is the best revenge.
—Anonymous

Because we're human, and thus imperfect beings, we'll often be less than serene. In fact, tension and upset may commonly characterize us. However, the anger or resentment we too frequently feel toward others generally causes the greatest harm to our own lives. Although we may wish ill to others, it returns, like a boomerang, to ourselves.

We let others assume command over our lives when we give energy to our resentments. Those who are the objects of our focus gradually control all of our moves. We are no longer free to grow, to determine our actions, when we have given over our power to those we resent. Our attention goes toward them, and we forsake the steps toward our personal goals that need to be taken.

Wanting revenge is human, though always unproductive. We should understand, however, that those who have triggered our anger have garnered the greatest revenge. They've managed to pull us off course. It's up to us to take back our power and go about our lives with joy and direction. How much sweeter is this response to the ones who deserve our greatest consideration: ourselves.

Today I'll live well and productively; having a resentment is a choice that I never need to make.

November 28

> *It is only by forgetting yourself that you draw near to God.*
>
> —*Henry David Thoreau*

There is a spiritual presence which can aptly cushion our every fall, bringing comfort and subtle meaning to our lives. However, we'll not feel this gentle comfort unless we attune ourselves to the others in our company. It's within another's soul that we sense the beacon of light which illuminates the way we're traveling.

Broadening our vision so that we may see life from a stranger's perspective heightens the clarity of our own, and sharing the view bonds us, deepens all meaning, and closes the gap that lies between.

We must think and dream beyond ourselves if we are ever to sense the vast network that includes us all. We can be certain there is a rhythm to the unfolding of our experiences; a symphony which knows its own end.

Today, I'll listen to the notes of others, and find my harmony with them.

*If you have been put in your place long
enough, you begin to act like the place.*
—*Randall Jarrell*

Others can't put us in our place all by themselves; we have to go there. Our cooperation is
required for snubs or blame or for glorification.
If we don't choose to accept the role another
has found for us, we don't have to play it.

Sometimes it's difficult to accept the choices
life offers us. It seems easier to go along with
the roles that others assign. How many people
do we know who seem to drift through important areas of their lives, neither fully cooperat-
ing nor asserting their own choices? They might
not like to admit it, but in "going along," they've
accepted someone else's definition of who they
are.

Some of us comply out of a desire to cooperate—but there's a big difference. Compliance
means refusing to exercise our own power to
choose; cooperation means using our power
together with others to achieve more than any
of us can alone. If we accept the responsibility
for our lives, we forego the luxury of saying,
"Look what you made me do;" but in exchange
we may get to do what we want.

*I will remember that anything that happens between us is
half mine and half yours.*

November 30

> *He who does not start life well will finish badly, one can tell.*
> — Great Calendar of 1500, quoted by
> Philippe Aries

As a species, we're obsessed with the future. We spend time, energy, and money on horoscopes, almanacs, and sophisticated statistical "predictors," all of which, we think, will enable us to foretell the future. But life, economics, and the weather resist most of our efforts to control them.

In the case of children, predictions are more complicated. If a child's parents decide "this one's going to be a loser," that child has a lot of overcoming to do.

Can we escape the noose of a self-fulfilling prediction? Yes, probably. Health, self-respect, and a balanced outlook are easier to achieve for us if we have had loving nurturance and support in early life. But even if our early life has been filled with neglect or abuse, we can learn to love and nurture ourselves. And we can pass along the blessing by refusing to predict the future for others in ways that damage or confine them.

All we really have is here and now. All we can control is our own behavior. When we surrender to these limits on our human power, we can begin to tap the sources of a power greater than ourselves.

I will surrender to the moment today.

December

The still mind of the sage is a mirror of heaven and earth—the glass of all things.
                                        —*Chuang Tzu*

In our own personal stillness, we find the solutions to the challenges facing us. We need to be willing to be quiet and turn our attention inward. No information we need eludes us for long when we dwell in the stillness.

Our opportunities for growth are hidden within the challenges that attract our attention. We need these if we are to contribute to the world. No challenge is beyond our capabilities or strength, and every one can be handled with relative ease if we have sought the comfort of the stillness.

The wisdom we admire in others is the birthright of us all. Each of us is a channel to full knowledge; any of us may be gifted with the wisdom to understand the present clearly, if we choose to exercise the commitment to move within ourselves—to the stillness, to the heart of all knowledge of the past, the present, and the future.

I'll have the answers I need, when I need them, if I turn within for them.

December 2

> *We should have much peace if we would not busy ourselves with the sayings and doings of others.*
>
> —Thomas À Kempis

We can go forth peacefully today if we pay close attention to our inner urgings; they will direct our steps safely and justly. The choice is forever ours to respect this inner voice—rather than be nudged off course or have our progress severely hindered by the strength of another's self-serving tug.

Action which is clearly our own, rather than reaction to another's laments, is certain to bring personal satisfaction. This will strengthen even more the connection between the self we offer to the world and the voice that nurtures, guides and safeguards us from within.

With practice we will develop an appreciation for all the people in our lives, and yet be free of their influence when it's not complementary to our own efforts. Taking full responsibility for who we are and where we're going is exhilarating. But even more, it's the only way we're certain of arriving at our most meaningful destination.

I will listen to and respect the men and women I meet today, but I will be most attentive to the friend within.

The first element of greatness is fundamental humbleness.

—Margot Asquith

Recognition of the magnitude of creation heightens our awareness of the small but essential contribution that we each offer to the whole. We come to know that we are necessary to *its* completion, thus we are special. With that knowledge we are quieted, softened, and secure. We are at peace.

Sensing the meaning of our own existence enlightens us about others' value as well. This knowledge fosters love, respect, and acceptance of another's unique personhood. Each attempt at nurturing another is, in turn, an act of self-nurture.

The road stretching before us looks long and will often be rocky. We'll inch along at times. But when we remember our value, our unique necessity to the whole, the rocks will easily be sidestepped and our pace will quicken.

I will breathe deeply the realization of my meaning today. I am needed by the people I meet. And I will recognize their value to me.

December 4

We are a feelingless people. If we could really feel, the pain would be so great that we would stop all the suffering.

—Julian Beck

Other people's suffering is painful to us; but we have skins that protect us from the continual awareness of pain. We know that we are connected to all other life forms on the planet; yet we are distinct beings who can disregard the suffering of the torture victim, the slaughtered animal, or the starving child.

The thickness of our skins is good in one sense; it lets some of us be whole and happy in a world where many are not. But if it is too thick, we become callous. We shut out reality and pretend—successfully, sometimes—that everyone is as well off as we are.

It's difficult to respond to the suffering of others in a balanced way. The Serenity Prayer can show us how:

Grant me the serenity to accept the
    things I cannot change;
Courage to change the things I can;
And wisdom to know the difference.

Much suffering can be lightened. Many decide to work, in some way, for the welfare of others. Our "feelinglessness" is only as deep as we decide.

My skin is a membrane that receives information from both sides. I will pay attention to both kinds of messages today.

At every step the child should be allowed to meet the real experiences of life; the thorns should never be plucked from the roses.
—Ellen Key

Reality is not always pleasant. More often it's painful. Accepting that pain, as well as pleasure, is part of the process of growth evens our responses to their presence in our daily lives. Being shielded or shielding another from pain directly hinders the rapture of pleasure.

Maturity is measurable by our response to the ebb and flow of the day, the season, even our lifetime. The vibrancy of life lies in the truth of experience. Myriad opportunities for growth, for rapture, for pensive meditation will present themselves every day. Absorbing from every experience will strengthen our character and prepare us for whatever lies ahead.

We cannot hide from pain. And we can grow from pain, whenever it appears.

Today may offer me pleasure and also pain. I need experiences of both to meet tomorrow.

December 6

Women who have reached positions of prominence . . . have not always been the best supporters of new measures to encourage female activism.
— Anna Coote and Beatrix Campbell

Generosity is a problem for some; they feel resentful. Giving to others seems unfair to them: "Nobody gave anything to me," they'll say. "I had to fight for everything I got." As if that were a reason to deny others.

Giving to others takes nothing away from us; on the contrary, it refreshes the soul. Yet the fear that someone else's success will mean our failure can keep us resentful and competitive.

Competition is drummed into us as children. It's a hard lesson to unlearn. But there aren't many traits that are so unsuitable—and so frustrating—as cutthroat competition. The person who must compete is doomed to unhappiness and to a sense of inadequacy. We'll stop the hopeless attempt to best others only when we achieve the serenity of knowing that each of us is the best at one thing: being ourselves.

Being the best me I can often involves my helping others.

December 7

*Every worthwhile accomplishment, big or
little, has its stages of drudgery and triumph;
a beginning, a struggle, and a victory.*
— *Anonymous*

Every goal that offers us pleasure on completion has triggered periods of pain. The lessons
we need to learn are seldom simple. Nonethe-
less, our development has relied on successfully
tackling them. We can be certain that goals we
are inspired to set for ourselves are tied closely
to the lessons we're in this life to learn.

It's not unusual for us to want an easier life,
one free from turmoil and pain. We'd rather not
know that a life with no bumps falls short of
the fulfillment we desire. But it does. We need
struggles to stretch our capabilities. We need
sorrow to appreciate the laughter. We need
boredom to discover joy in small blessings.

Every worthy task will avail us of opportunities to grow, to think new thoughts and to
hone the skills we already possess. Every worthy
task is destined to clear new ground for us.

*Today I can celebrate, I'm on the road to victory. Every
step leads toward the goal I've chosen.*

December 8

Alienation is essentially experiencing the world and oneself passively, receptively, as the subject separated from the object.
—Erich Fromm

The goal of our spiritual quest is to put ourselves back together, reintegrating the self that acts and the self that observes. To be split is to be in pain. We feel our inner separation as a wound, and we try to dull our pain with frantic or self-destructive methods.

The pain won't yield to pleasure, nor to danger or violence. These sensational methods leave us as alienated as we were before. We seek wholeness, and we'll achieve it only by surrendering to our sense of a reality beyond ourselves. Whatever we choose to call the great oneness, we must acknowledge it as a higher power or we'll continue to suffer the anguish of alienation.

Achieving serenity is a lifelong process. While we have this goal in view, our efforts will be unified and our attention not easily distracted by setbacks.

Today I'll resolve to focus on my spiritual goal and let it heal me.

*When you hold resentment toward another,
you are bound to that person or condition
by an emotional link that is stronger than
steel.*
                              —Catherine Ponder

Our attention is consumed by what we want
to control. Like a magnet, we are attracted to
it; preoccupation sets in, and our freedom to
live in the moment is gone. We give up living
when we try to control others.

Our resentments grow out of our failure to
control others, a failure that heightens our
personal insecurities. When we need others to
fall into line, to buy our plan, we have set ourselves up for failure. We have guaranteed that
we'll experience the feelings of inadequacy that
we dread.

Each one of us is on a path that is landscaped
according to our inner needs. Accepting that
will relieve us of the anger triggered when other
people behave according to their own dictates
rather than ours.

Resentment stifles us. To respond creatively
to the fluctuation of the day, we need to make
the most of our personal power.

*Let me follow my path today, knowing it's right for me.
I will work on letting others walk their own paths, too.*

December 10

*Eternity is called whole, not because it has
parts, but because it is lacking in nothing.*
— *Thomas Aquinas*

We all learn in geometry that the circle is a
perfect form, but there's no such thing as a
perfect circle. Straight lines aren't perfectly
straight; a flat floor can never be perfectly flat.
Perfection is an idea that can never be realized.

The idea of eternity is beautiful, like the idea
of perfection. It expresses the striving of the
human spirit for perfect unity; the fulfillment,
the perfect satisfaction, of all desire, perfect
wholeness, "lacking in nothing."

Of course, eternity is an impossible standard
to attain. Civilizations aren't eternal, nor are
laws, nor works of art. We make ourselves miserable if we try to measure our achievements
against such a standard. We invent techniques
and gadgets to help us overcome our human
weakness and awkwardness. And we cooperate
with others, both weaker and stronger than
ourselves, to multiply our efforts manyfold.
How much kinder it would be to love the idea,
as an expression of longing, and to love ourselves because we do the best we can. It's because we lack many things that human beings
are so creative and ingenious.

*My fullest expression of myself is in my reaching out
to others.*

It is not often given in a noisy world to come
to the places of great grief and silence.
                              —*Sarah Orne Jewett*

Many of us live with energy and gusto, tackling our lives like wrestling partners, busy earning a living, caring for our homes and families, serving our communities. Are we forgetting something?

Often, we forget to nourish our spirits at the deep well of grief and silence. Grief is a nourishing emotion, because in grieving we experience fully the inevitable losses of our lives. Only after grieving can we heal. Only after knowing fully the dimensions of our loss can we summon the vitality to continue our lives.

Parents, friends, children, trusted leaders die and cannot be replaced. Their loss may have deep meaning for us; we deserve to take the time and care to learn what that meaning may be.

Grief can change people; we may become more detached, quieter, more feeling, more deeply appreciative of life's gifts. One of these gifts is silence—the silence of tranquility. Through plumbing our feelings, we may come to be at peace.

Not all gifts are gaiety, love, and joy. Let me respect the
gifts of grief and silence, that I may learn from them.

December 12

Pain is inevitable. Suffering is optional.
— *M. Kathleen Casey*

Every day is a series of experiences; some we'll greet with relief, laughter, or anger. However, all experiences, even those most dreaded, encompass the very lessons we're ready to undertake. And the people in our lives are here to serve as our mentors.

The pinch of any experience lives on in the mind. We sometimes savor the wound, letting it feed our self-pity or fester our resentment. Likewise, we often hang on to a fond memory, replaying the action over and over again in our minds. Whether it's a good or a bad memory, we neglect the present if our minds are locked in to the past.

Our freedom to let go of an experience, to laugh at ourselves, to accentuate the positive in our lives, exhilarates us. It also heightens our anticipation for every moment a day promises.

I am personally in charge of my responses to all experiences today. I can feel however I choose every minute of the day.

December 13

In crowded courts I find myself alone,
And pay my worship to a nobler throne,
Long since the value of this world I know,
Pity the madness, and despise the show. . . .
    —Lady Mary Wortley Montagu

Some people seem to be able to hold two separate scales of value, one labeled "Eternal" and one labeled "Worldy." The "Eternal" scale features values like truth, peace, love; the "Worldly" scale is notched at more concrete marks of success: car, boat, jewels, executive directorship.

There is nothing wrong with worldly success, unless we pretend that these two scales are unconnected. Eternal values are just that: enduring qualities that time can't change. Compared to them, worldly success is trivial. Where we sometimes go wrong is in pursuing the trivial aims at the expense of the enduring ones.

The key to a successful life must involve combining these scales. Insisting on a single standard of value will protect us from deluding ourselves about the values of worldly things and ensures that whatever we achieve is truly worthwhile. The true riches of the spirit are within our grasp.

If I have a double standard of success, I'm fooling myself. I'll be true to my real values.

December 14

The cruelest lies are often told in silence.
                    —Robert Louis Stevenson

Is it frequent that we fail to come forth to explain, defend, or offer support? Remaining silent is always our option, no matter how grave the situation. Holding back information that would ease another's pain or shed light on a hateful experience is cruel. The effects of cruel acts will find their way back to the actor. The axiom, "As we sow so shall we reap" is true.

Perhaps we need reminding that our performance is unique and essential to those around us. Together we move forward, in concert. When any one of us falters or misses a cue, another of us will likely miss one, too.

We're alive to honor one another's presence, and only when we're fully present, honest, and straightforward, are we fulfilling our role.

Today I share center stage. Let me speak my lines fully.

*Eat and carouse with Bacchus, or munch
dry bread with Jesus, but don't sit down
without one of the gods.*
                              —D. H. Lawrence

In religious communities, as in tribal societies, the ordinary events of life are sanctified. Orthodox Jews and Benedictine monks are alike in this, and so are devout Buddhists, Hindus, or animists. Prayer and ritual observance aren't reserved for special occasions; they accompany sleeping, waking, the daily washing of the body, the simplest meal.

Whatever our beliefs, it's possible for us to express the spiritual dimension of our lives in simple, everyday ways. And each expression strengthens our spirituality and extends it to flood more of our life with light. Whatever names we give to the truths of the spirits, our least act can connect us with them.

The stronger our spiritual connection, the less we'll be held back by our fears and self-doubts. If we can invoke a trusted guide for the ordinary gestures of life, then we'll never lack guidance in perplexity.

I will feed my spirit and it will grow strong.

December 16

> *Our awesome responsibility to ourselves, to
> our children, and to the future is to create
> ourselves in the image of goodness, because
> the future depends on the nobility of our
> imaginings.*
> —Barbara Grizzuti Harrison

The world we live in depends on the responsible contributions each of us makes. And this world is just as good as are the many talents we commit ourselves to developing and offering. None of us is without obligation to offer our best to our family, friends, or strangers, if our hope is to live in a good world. The world can only be as good as each of us make it.

Individually and collectively our power to mold the outer circumstances of our lives is profound. Our personal responses to one another and our reactions to events that touch us combine with the actions of others to create a changed environment that affects us. No action, no thought goes unnoticed, unfelt, in this interdependent system of humanity. We share this universe. We are the force behind all that the universe offers.

*Whether I acknowledge the depth of my contribution is
irrelevant. It is still profound and making an impact
every moment and eternally.*

Some things you must always be unable to bear.

— *William Faulkner*

The strong spirit cannot bear lies; the free spirit cannot bear shackles. To tend our spirit with love and rigor means weeding it like a garden, cleaning it of false values and fake pride. We must never bear those things that violate our integrity.

Sometimes, for the sake of peace or a secret doubt that we deserve excellence, we violate ourselves. We give away pieces of our truth and we tell ourselves it doesn't matter. But it does. And we deserve excellence; we deserve the best quality of life. Peace bought at the price of spiritual violation is no true peace; it is a form of oppression.

Meditation can strengthen the spirit against violation. Today and every day, we will practice becoming the person we deserve to be.

When I listen to my own truth I will be guided truly.

December 18

> . . . I am incapable of conceiving infinity,
> and yet I do not accept finity. I want this ad-
> venture that is the context of my life to go on
> without end.
>
> —Simone de Beauvoir

The paradox of life is that we cannot conceive of its ending, but we also can't conceive of its not ending. We have the image of the circle to help us out of this dilemma. And if we think of the vast cycles of time and generation, the image of a spiral comes to mind.

The rich web, the adventure of life, goes on without end. It preceded us and will outlast us, and humans will go on struggling and surrendering. A related paradox is that we live in a moment of time that is constantly becoming the past, yet will affect a future that we cannot really predict or control. All we have to work with is our brief arc of life, now.

Yet how precious it is, and how vast, and how it is extended by our ties with others. The web of our relatedness to others brings us into their lives, them into ours. As we share our attention, we enrich our spirits, and we're enriched again by the gifts of others.

A further paradox: every individual is alone, yet none of us is unaccompanied on the curving journey that takes us through this life.

Only by letting go of life do I most profoundly enhance it.

*Gift, like genius, I often think only means
an infinite capacity for taking pains.*
— *Jane Ellice Hopkins*

There is no easy way through this life. Few days are void of struggle. Some days are fraught with it. Each day presses us in some manner. Our opportunities for growth, whether on the job or in relationships, are generally accompanied by the pinch of a difficult decision or the push of an unwelcome thought.

Often we need reminding that we're unlikely to attain personal growth without the experience of pain. Pain first beckons and then pushes us forward to new solutions for tired, old situations. But these new solutions will always surface if we trust ourselves to move through the pain.

No problem is beyond solving. The process of living, when experienced with care and patience, will reveal the solution that any problem contains.

*I will take today slowly and easily. If a struggle develops,
I will cherish it. It means growth.*

December 20

> *Injustice anywhere is a threat to justice every-where. We are caught in an inescapable net-work of mutuality, tied in a single garment of destiny.*
>
> —*Martin Luther King*

Safe in our own homes, or deep into our jobs, it's difficult to remember that we're part of the indivisible life of each, and that everything we do affects that "network of mutuality," just as we're affected by it. Stop and think of the beautiful image of the Arctic tundra, or the atmospheric envelope. These are parts of the world that we may have thought of as inert, nonliving, until we learned how delicate is their sensitivity to everything that touches them.

And everything touches them, as everything touches us. We are as much a part of the rhythm of life as the delicate web of roots that hold the permafrost in place. The same over-arching world spirit inhabits us, and we are as necessary as molecules of oxygen.

At last, we have achieved the capacity to communicate with our fellow human beings. Let us hope we can do it as well as sparrows do, or grass, for we can shape our destiny even as we're shaped by it.

I will try to live today so as to answer for it to all my fellow creatures.

Now in the middle of my days I glean
this truth that has a flower's freshness:
life is the gold and sweetness of wheat,
hate is brief and love immense.
                              —Gabriella Mistral

Eternal truths are always fresh. That's why so many people treasure a daily spiritual guide as an occasion for meditation. Each day we can refresh our spirits with the help of such a guide.

Meditation is a process of simplifying, emptying out, concentrating our minds. We won't achieve much spiritual progress from simply reading these words; they're just the beginning, just the signpost. Growth comes from the work we do, transforming spiritual nourishment into the strength we need.

Some of us are skeptical at first. We don't believe we need to acquire any more disciplines; our spirits are in fine shape, thanks very much. But then we notice a change in our friends or intimates; they've made a discovery. Mysteriously, their lives are straightening out. Maybe we ought to try some of whatever they've got.

It doesn't matter how we come to a program of spiritual growth. The truth was here all the time, waiting for us.

I can't speak the truth too often; it's new every day.

December 22

> *Whensoever a man desires anything inordinately, he is presently disquieted within himself.*
>
> —*Thomas À Kempis*

We are at peace when we cherish the gifts of the present moment. And gratitude for the moment enhances the value of what is to come next. When we take our focus off the present, longing only for another time or place or experience, we'll never reap the rewards that offer themselves to us moment by moment. The longing heart guarantees little peace, infrequent moments of joy, and stunted growth. The soul's nourishment is here, now, with these people who surround us and within these activities inviting our involvement.

So few people understand the benefits of celebrating life as it's received. Finding pleasure in the ordinary occurrences heightens our awareness that indeed, no occurrence is truly ordinary. Every moment is special.

I can answer yes to today and all it offers, and be at peace.

Women and men in the crowd meet and
mingle.
Yet with itself every soul standeth single.
— Alice Carey

Joy for living depends on the level of intimacy
with others that we've grown comfortable with:
sharing our grief, our fears, and our glories
with others relieves their power over us and
fosters a healthier perspective on all the situations in our lives. Yet, even the deepest level of
sharing doesn't relieve us of the need to come
to full acceptance, solely alone, of the turmoil,
the trauma, the tension in our lives.

Interdependently we share this universe,
each of us giving to its continuance and receiving sustenance in turn. With little thought,
really, we are living our lives bonded in myriad
ways, great and small, to one another and to the
cycles of the earth housing us all. Just as absolute as is our interdependence, so sure is our
need to be at peace. This means to be alone, but
not lonely, with our soul's relentless search for
understanding, for serenity, for certainty about
the direction we are taking. Together and yet
alone we are traveling the path of life.

*I will find a listener today if I want closeness with someone.
And I'll need time alone, away, to understand the life I've
been given.*

December 24

> . . . (To) take something from yourself, to give
> to another, that is humane and gentle and
> never takes away as much comfort as it brings
> again.
>
> —Thomas More

We take different kinds of pleasure in giving. Perhaps the purest is the gift to a child so young it doesn't really know who the gift came from; the pure joy that the teddy bear or pull-toy produces is our reward, unmixed by any expectation of return.

When children get older, we want something back from them: gratitude, respect. The gift is less pure. When lovers exchange gifts, their pleasure is often tinged with anxiety: Did I give more than I got? Did I get more than I gave? Or with power: He'll always remember where he got that shirt; she owes me something for the fur jacket.

To friends and relations our gifts reflect many things: our appreciation of their lives, our shared memories, our prosperity. We tend to give in a spirit of *self*-expression.

Perhaps the closest we can come to a pure gift is an anonymous one: a gift of volunteer work, of blood, or a contribution to a charity. Such a gift, which can never be acknowledged or returned by those it comforts, can heal our spirits when they are wearied by too much ego.

The gift of *myself can be a gift* to *myself.*

*That life is a fragile shell on the beach I have
thought of before. This Christmas I am thinking big basic wonders as if I were just born.*
— *Naomi Shihab Nye*

The big basic wonders about our origin, and
that of the stars, must still occur to us all, even
though we're grown up and knowledgeable
about astronomy and human reproduction.
The germination of a seed is still much more
wonderful, in a strict sense, than the mere elec-
tronic marvel of a calculator that makes twelve
thousand computations in a second.

Do we ever let ourselves simply wonder? Do
we still open ourselves to the awe that filled us
once, when we first realized the vast intricacies
of the solar system or of human physiology?

Every great ritual surrounds a story that is
wonderful: the presence of a god; the deliverance of a people; the transformation of life
or death. It's appropriate that we should respond
to them with a thrill of wonder. Wonder is a
gift; it contains the germs of reverence and of
knowledge.

*Life is frail and intricate, and it contains everything I
need for fulfillment.*

December 26

A holiday is a permitted—or rather a prescribed—excess, a solemn violation of a prohibition.

— Sigmund Freud

Breaking our own small rules is a luxury that we sometimes forget to indulge. How pleasant it can be to stay in bed late on a Sunday, not get dressed or shaved, to let clutter accumulate. On our days off, we can get a thrill from such "solemn violations" as going to a film in the afternoon, eating an unscheduled treat, jogging twice around the track.

It's probably important to give ourselves these little extravagances, especially if our usual lives involve a highly organized routine. Just breaking up the day differently—reversing daytime and nighttime activities for example—can give a special flavor to a day off.

Routine is consoling for many of us. We feel good about ourselves as long as we keep to the schedule, obey the rules. But we need to break some rules to get a different kind of good feeling about ourselves; above all, to know that we can choose to return to our former law-abiding selves. Sometimes we fear that if we step out of line once, we'll never get our lives together again. We need to know that we can renew ourselves on a holiday.

Giving myself a holiday by breaking my routine can make it stronger—because I choose to resume it.

December 27

*Anger repressed can poison a relationship as
surely as the cruelest words.*
>   —Joyce Brothers

Anger toward a mate, a coworker, a friend,
or neighbor, builds a strong wall, separating us
from everyone if we don't acknowledge the
cause of the anger. Like any secret, denied anger
festers and infects relations with friends, acquaintances, even strangers. It dominates our
attention and pollutes every emotion. But more
importantly, if not checked it controls us, and
this all-consuming power then decides our
destiny.

Anger doesn't need to be a major force in our
life. Like any emotion, we can learn from it, but
we must let it go if we are to grow. It helps to
remember the sweet aftertaste when an angry
encounter is resolved.

Anger acknowledged and resolved tightens
understanding between people, and encourages
intimacy. Anger is bittersweet when squarely
faced.

My anger need not own me today.

December 28

*How magnificently you tossed away this God
who plagues and helps man so much! But you
did not and could not toss out of your heart
that part of you from which the God notion
had come.*

—Richard Wright

Each of us accommodates "the God notion"
in our own way, but we all have it. Although we
may not all worship a great Mother or Father
figure, our spiritual dimension makes us all kin.

To deny our spiritual selves will bring us un-
rest; our life's journey is always toward serenity,
and serenity means finding peace within, an-
swering those searching questions of the spirit.
Some of us will seek answers in many forms, in
different languages, but our quest is as real and
as simple if we stay at home and explore within
ourselves.

When we're honest with ourselves, we find
this radiant truth: an authentic search for spiritual wholeness can be successful.

*Let me honor "the God notion" and never use it against
myself or any fellow being.*

The way in which we think of ourselves has
everything to do with how our world sees us
and how we can see ourselves successfully
acknowledged by that world.
                                    —Arlene Raven

Our self-perception determines how we present ourselves. The posture we've assumed invites others' praise, interest, or criticism. What others think of us accurately reflects our personal self-assessment, a message we've conveyed directly or subtly.

It behooves us to acknowledge the power we each master over others' judgements and opinions of our worth. It's with absolute certainty that those opinions are molded by our own. When our personal opinions are negative, it's likely to be because we've lost touch with the rhythm of this life we're sharing with others. Perhaps we've forgotten what is essential to the completion of the whole. Perhaps a gentle reminder is needed, day by day.

How I grade myself today will be imitated by the men and women who share my experiences. I can earn high marks if I want to.

December 30

> . . . Is not all the world beyond these four
> little walls pitiless enough, but that thou
> must need enter here—thou, O Death?
> —W.E.B. Du Bois

The concept of a refuge strengthens us. For
some of us, it's a dark basement and head-
phones, or a workbench; for others, a garden or
a bedroom.

Some of us take refuge outside ourselves, in
our spiritual faith. There we find a death-
defying certainty and a reminder that our being
is a gift. Some of us find this refuge in service
to others; we feel the benign power of creation
stream through us, and we're strengthened.

Death is part of life, and it belongs on the same
plane as life's other events: birth, nurturing, and
sickness. But spiritual refuge lifts us to another
plane, where the powers of life and death join to
form the whole of existence. This higher truth,
like all real refuge, lies within us. We can summon it as the need arises.

*The more I turn outward to others, the stronger I become
within.*

December 31

Despite my geographical love of mankind,
I would be attacked by local fears.
                                    —Grace Paley

We may have the highest principles, be generous, trusting, and public-spirited, and still find ourselves assailed at times by doubts and fears. The "local fears" don't mean that we've betrayed our "geographical" principles; only that, this time, we're afraid.

The wonderful thing about being human is that we can choose how we act at any given moment. If we find ourselves behaving in a way we don't like, we can choose to change; either to change our behavior or—if that doesn't seem possible—to change the way we look at it. It's wisely said: "You can do something for twelve hours that you could never think of doing your whole life long."

It's a waste of time and effort to disapprove of ourselves. If we won't change our behavior, let's change our standards. Many of us have impossibly high expectations for ourselves, and when we don't measure up, we feel guilty.

Guilt is unproductive. When we keep everything in the moment—the "geographical" as well as the "local"—we can accept ourselves as we are. We are as good, right now, as we can be.

Scaling down my expectations closer to what I'm capable of will aid my spiritual growth.

SUBJECT INDEX

AUTHOR INDEX

Beck, Julian . . . . Dec. 4
Beerbohm, Max . . . . . June 13
Behn, Aphra . . . . May 5
Belmont, Eleanor R. . . . Jan. 10
Benedict, Ruth . . . . . . Feb. 6
Bengis, Ingrid . . . . . . May 26, Oct. 10
Berger, John . . . . June 23
Bergler, Edmund . . . . . June 20
Bernikov, Louise . . . . . Jan. 19
Betts, George . . . . . . Nov. 4
Blackwell, Elizabeth . . . April 10
Blake, William . . . . . . Jan. 28
Bly, Robert . . . . Sept. 15, Oct. 1
Boesing, Martha . . . . . July 25
Bogan, Louise . . . . . . Jan. 14
"Box-Car Bertha" . . . . Oct. 12
Braddon, Mary Elizabeth . July 2
Brainard, Joe . . . . . . Feb. 7
Branch, Anna Hempstead . Nov. 1
Brancusi, Konstantin . . . Nov. 19
Bronte, Charlotte . . . . Sept. 6
Brooks, Cleanth . . . . . June 1
Brooks, Gwendolyn . . . Sept. 23
Brothers, Joyce . . . . . Dec. 27
Browne, Sir Thomas . . . May 21
Browning, ... May 31
   Elizabeth Barrett
Bryant, Dorothy . . . . . Nov. 3
Buck, Pearl S. . . . . . . Jan. 1, April 20
Burton, Robert . . . . . May 17
Buscaglia, Leo F. . . . . . Sept. 9
Camus, Albert . . . . . . June 15
Carey, Alice . . . . Dec. 23

Hazelden
Always, the pioneer

Other daily meditation books that may interest you...

Each Day a New Beginning

The first daily meditation guide created by and for women involved in 12-Step recovery programs. Nearly 200,000 women have found help in this collection of thoughts and reflections that offers hope, strength, and guidance every day of the year. Our number two bestseller. (400 pp.)

Order No. 1076A

Food For Thought

A daily meditation book for the recovering compulsive overeater written with the sensitivity and insight that only a fellow member in the O.A. program could provide. Written in the tradition of the very popular *Twenty-Four Hours a Day*, this book is among our top ten best-sellers, with over 100,000 copies sold. (365 pp.)

"Every morning I read Food For Thought. *For me, it's a livesaver. I don't know what I'd do without it -- I really need it to help me stay abstinent."*
Lisa A. -- MN.

Order No. 1074A

For price and order information, please call one of our Customer Service Representatives.

Hazelden
Educational Materials

Box 176, Center City, MN 55012
(800) 328-9000 (Toll Free. Cont. U.S. Only.)
(800) 328-0500 (Toll Free. Film and Video Orders. Cont. U.S. Only.)
464-8844 (Toll Free. Metro Twin Cities.)
(612) 257-4010 (MN & Outside Cont. U.S.)

Order No. 1045